SELECTED POEMS OF EDITH WHARTON

EDITH WHARTON

IRENE GOLDMAN-PRICE, EDITOR

SCRIBNER

NEW YORK LONDON TORONTO SYDNEY NEW DELHI

Scribner
An Imprint of Simon & Schuster, Inc.
1230 Avenue of the Americas
New York, NY 10020

First Scribner trade paperback edition July 2019

SCRIBNER and design are registered trademarks of The Gale Group, Inc.,
used under license by Simon & Schuster, Inc., the publisher of this work.

For information about special discounts for bulk purchases, please contact Simon & Schuster
Special Sales at 1-866-506-1949 or business@simonandschuster.com.

The Simon & Schuster Speakers Bureau can bring authors to your live event.
For more information or to book an event contact the Simon & Schuster Speakers Bureau
at 1-866-248-3049 or visit our website at www.simonspeakers.com.

Interior design by Kyle Kabel

Manufactured in the United States of America

1   3   5   7   9   10   8   6   4   2

Library of Congress Cataloging-in-Publication Data

Names: Wharton, Edith, 1862-1937, author. | Goldman-Price, Irene C., editor.
Title: Selected poems of Edith Wharton / Edith Wharton ; Irene Goldman-Price, editor.
Description: New York, NY : Scribner, 2019. | Series: Scribner fiction original trade |
Includes bibliographical references.
Identifiers: LCCN 2019008618 (print) | LCCN 2019016340 (ebook) |
ISBN 9781501182846 | ISBN 9781501182839 | ISBN 9781501182839
(paperback : alk. paper) | ISBN 9781501182846 (ebook)
Subjects: LCSH: American poetry—19th century. | American poetry—20th century.
Classification: LCC PS3545.H16 (ebook) | LCC PS3545.H16 A6 2019 (print) |
DDC 811/.52—dc23
LC record available at https://lccn.loc.gov/2019008618

ISBN 978-1-5011-8283-9
ISBN 978-1-5011-8284-6 (ebook)

For Susan Wissler,
who has for many years given of her time and
abundant talent to honor Edith Wharton's legacy.

Contents

ARRESTING CHARACTERS 145

THE ART OF POETRY 215

Introduction

Words, words pursue me with their cadences,
Like birds that babble in the woods at dawn,
Flitting now this, now that way thro' the trees,
Now flashing forth, now swift again withdrawn—

—Edith Wharton, Lilly poetry notebook

A t a dinner party one evening, seated next to the philosopher Henri Bergson, Edith Wharton lamented "odd holes" in her memory. How was it that she could remember a variety of useless and insignificant things, she asked him, but when it came to poetry, her "chiefest passion and . . . greatest joy," her verbal memory failed completely, and she heard "only the inner cadence, and could hardly ever fill it out with the right words"? Bergson replied rather matter-of-factly: he said it was simply because she was dazzled. Great poetry can evoke an emotional response beyond words. Wharton concluded that the best definition of poetry was "the gift of precision in ecstasy," the gift of finding the exact right words to express the ineffable (*A Backward Glance* 170).

Wharton loved words even before she could read them. In the autobiographical fragment "Life and I," she divulged being "enthralled" by the sound of words, whether she understood them or not; being "intoxicated" by meter, and enjoying a "sensuous rapture" from the sound and the sight of words on the page. Her desire to make up stories became a "devastating passion," a "perilous obsession." Savoring the sounds of words apart from their meaning, she felt their rhythms and she attended to the color and expressiveness of each word (1074–76).

As a mature writer, Wharton studied etymology and grammar and she took pleasure in dissecting words. Her friend Logan Pearsall Smith, an essayist and philologist, once remarked: "Fine writers should split hairs together, sit side by side, like friendly apes, to pick the fleas from each other's fur" (*Afterthoughts* 55). While one can't quite see Edith Wharton in a party of apes, one can certainly imagine her among her guests of an evening, relaxing in the library and pondering the fine points of such terms as "inspiration," "fancy," and "imagination," terms she and Smith debated while cruising the Aegean in 1926. That conversation led Wharton to change the name of her paean to her imagination from "The Comrade" to "La Folle du Logis," an old French term for the way imagination feels like a madman in your house. Words—like paint or clay or marble to a studio artist—were the medium in which she could express her inner world.

What was the nature of that inner world? As an adult her language for the experience of reading and creating was as violent and passionate as if she were still a teenager: "intoxicated," "teeming visions," "volcanic eruptions," "sensuous rapture," "ecstasy." The words suggest that her feelings about her imagination were distinctly mixed. "Perilous obsession" intimates a lack of control that is compelling yet dangerous. And the term "furious Muse" embraces contradictory mythical allusions. The Muses, daughters of the great god Zeus and Mnemosyne, goddess of memory, were said to inspire artists. But the Furies, heads wreathed with serpents, chased down those who had broken the laws, relentless in their pursuit of punishment for the guilty. By calling her propelling force the "furious Muse," Wharton evokes the tension within her of being nurtured by the Muses while at the same time being hounded by the Furies (Wharton, "Life and I" 1074–76; *A Backward Glance* 35, 197, 200).

This creative drive, described hauntingly in her poems "La Folle du Logis" and "Life [Nay, lift me to thy lips]," manifests most strongly in Wharton's poetry. Looking at her notebooks one sees that the Wharton who wrote stories and novels, the witty, satiric Wharton who created characters from two or three of their foibles, was only one layer of a rich personality. Her fiction allowed her to explore relations among people in a realistic social world, usually with irony and humor. But the land of her poems is deeper, more heartfelt, and quite different from the land of her stories. It is a romantic place, sublime, mythic, and often painful. Poetry allowed her to explore her intimate feelings and the darker reaches of her prodigious imagination.

Along with imagination, Wharton knew that writing poetry required serious work. On the first page of her poetry notebook, created when she was in her thirties, are inscribed these words from "L'art," by Théophile Gautier: "*Sculpte, lime, cisèle,*" meaning, "sculpt, chisel, file." Art requires thinking, shaping, refining. She wrote to several aspiring poets about the need, in fully realized poetry, for expression, for finding the elegant, felicitous word to evoke in a reader a particular feeling or mood.

And for Wharton, the choice of word should be aided necessarily by a sense of sound and rhythm as much as if not more than by its meaning. She preferred the American poet Sidney Lanier's method of scansion using notes and rests, as if the line of poetry were a line of music, rather than the traditional stress and unstress markings that were derived from scanning Greek and Latin. An essential quality of Wharton's poems is their musicality: to get their full import one must read her poems aloud.

Wharton wrote poetry all of her life, amassing more than two hundred poems by the end. Her first publicly published work, at age seventeen, was "Only a Child," a poem about a boy who hanged himself in a Philadelphia house of refuge for vagrant children. She had read about the tragedy in the *New York World* and sent her poem the next day. It was hardly her first poem; a year earlier her parents had arranged for the private printing of twenty-nine poems garnered from their daughter's writings, which they called *Verses* (1878). Over the years Wharton continued to publish poetry in periodicals, and she also produced two more volumes: *Artemis to Actæon* (1909) and *Twelve Poems* (1926), for a lifetime publication of one hundred poems. Other poems were enclosed in letters, inscribed in books given to friends, and jotted down in her numerous diaries. In the papers left at her death we find a 168-page notebook filled with poems written in a fair hand and many more poems typed out as though readied for publication.

Poetry seems to have flowed most freely during five periods of her long life, beginning in youth. In the late nineteenth century, writing verse was the most acceptable form of writing for well-bred young ladies. Born into New York society in 1862, young Edith Jones sought to express herself in this conventional way, exploring her longings and frustrations, negotiating the rules for acceptable discourse and deportment, satirizing the behavior of those around her, and exploring religious matters and matters of life and death. During her early years, she was fortunate to have a governess who challenged her with reading German poetry as well as English. Because she lived in Europe from age four until age ten, young Edith also possessed an early command of Italian and French. And when the family returned to its New York home, she had access to her father's full library of history, philosophy, science, and literature. So she flexed her intellectual muscles: she translated poems from the German, Italian, and Old English, and she practiced verse forms from sonnets and ballads to terza rima and experiments in stress, rhyme, meter, and repetition. Her later poems demonstrate a long apprenticeship in prosody and a deep immersion in history, myth, and the natural sciences.

After her youthful experimentation with verse, in 1885 Edith Newbold Jones married the charming and eligible Bostonian Edward (Teddy) Wharton. He was more a sportsman than a literary man; they shared a love of travel and of outdoor activities like bicycling and ice skating. Nevertheless, he supported Puss (as the family called Edith) in her writing, which she began again about five or six years into their marriage. From 1889 to 1893 she filled that large poetry notebook, not with drafts but with finished poems written in her best hand. She published a few poems about history and art during those years, but soon she found her strongest voice as a novelist, storyteller, critic, and travel writer, all the work for which she would become most famous.

Some dozen years later, in her forties, after Teddy's deteriorating mental health became increasingly obvious and difficult, Wharton fell deeply in love with the American journalist William Morton Fullerton. For all his charms and talent Fullerton was, to use the language of the day, a cad. Just days before he began his flirtation with Wharton he had pledged his cousin Katharine Fullerton to a secret engagement, and he would keep her on a string for several years. He had been secretly married to one Frenchwoman and was living long-term with another, who was currently blackmailing him, threatening to expose his several homosexual affairs. He must have been magnetic, and Wharton was drawn, thrilled and anguished, into his orbit. This thralldom of love never quite fulfilled gave rise to dozens of poems, some of which she sent to him or recorded in a secret diary, and others she collected in her 1909 volume, *Artemis to Actæon*. In them we find as much pain as joy, almost as much death as life.

The Great War once again stimulated Wharton's poetic faculties. Living in Paris, she undertook both volunteer service and war journalism. Her experience of daily life in wartime Paris gave rise to fiction, including the undeservedly undervalued *A Son at the Front* (1923). Her articles written about travel to the war zone were collected in *Fighting France* (1915). She also wrote numerous poems: some patriotic, several elegies. In those poems one can observe her strong belief that the United States should involve itself in the war, and at the same time her own changing attitudes toward war from something glorious to a tragedy of families, villages, and the land destroyed, and young lives cut down.

A final flowering of poetry came when Wharton was in her sixties and seventies, traveling again to the Aegean Sea, enjoying the natural beauty of her beloved southern France and contemplating ultimate questions. Here she is at her most comfortable with both subject and technique. This is the poetry of a mature woman at peace with her world.

Early on, Wharton had been far from secure about her abilities as a poet, particularly in her thirties and forties. She demurred at the first request from Scribner's literary adviser and book editor William Crary Brownell to collect a volume, saying "there are degrees in prose and in poetry—below a certain point—well, it simply isn't poetry: and I am not sure I've ever reached the 'poetry line'" (EW to WCB, 6 November 1902, in Lewis and Lewis, *Letters of Edith Wharton* 75). Nevertheless, she was also ambitious. She wrote to another editor and friend, Richard Watson Gilder, thanking him for praising her poem "Life [Nay, lift me to thy lips]": "I'm rather self-critical about my prose, but my verse seems to get written by an 'alien energy,' and then I look at it helplessly, and wonder what it's like!" (EW to RWG, 3 November 1908, Benstock files, Scott Marshall Collection, The Mount). It seems as if she is disclaiming any ability to control or judge her composition; however, quoting Ralph Waldo Emerson's description of the process of thought—alien energy—from "The Over-Soul" places her in august company. And she does the same when she laments to Brownell that she can't find copies of her poems, that her verse is "fugitive," echoing the title of Byron's first volume of poetry, *Fugitive Pieces* (EW to WCB, 6 November 1902, in Lewis and Lewis, *Letters of Edith Wharton* 74–75). But her poems were not lost. She saved them, and she left us an abundant accumulation of poems to ponder and enjoy.

SELECTED for both representation and quality, here are some of her better-known poems along with previously unavailable texts written over the span of her life. Arranged thematically, they provide the opportunity to contemplate which subjects Wharton chose to explore in poetry rather than prose, as well as to consider how certain themes were handled at different times, in both poetry and prose. To orient the reader in time, the date or approximate date of composition is below each poem in brackets on the left. On the right, in parentheses, is the date of first publication. Each section has an introduction to the theme, and most poems are preceded by a brief contextual note. Wharton's preference for British spelling is retained, but her manuscript ampersands are replaced with "and." Readers have tended to ignore the impressive body of her verse in favor of her fiction, memoir, and writings about travel, gardening, and house decoration. This collection, which includes fifty poems never before published, encourages attention to Wharton as a poet and invites reevaluation.

SELECTED POEMS OF EDITH WHARTON

Edith Wharton at forty-eight, captured by the fashion photographer Peter Powel.

Landscapes of the Imagination

We have seen how intensely Wharton felt her imagination, how all-consuming it seemed to her. In "La Folle du Logis" she called it a "wild, wingèd thing," a "divine accomplice" perpetually inhabiting her; in her memoir it was a "furious Muse" that drove her to run away from other children so that she could "make up." Out of this cauldron of images, ideas, sounds, and words bubbled up her stories, novels, and plays. But it was in her poetry that she revealed the strangest, deepest visions that haunted her.

Inspired by history and myth as were the Romantic poets before her, Wharton sought sometimes to evoke the heroic past, sometimes to reveal an immaterial world beyond the physical. To paraphrase Walter Pater's description of Romantic poetry, she added strangeness to beauty in search of a way to convey the ineffable. Sounds, images, sensory experience, memory, and deep emotion all found expression in her poetry.

This group of poems centers on landscape, outer and inner. As a traveler, Wharton ruminated on the places she visited and reveled in imagining events that once unfolded in the landscape before her. Several poems here emerge from such contemplation. Interestingly, "Battle Sleep," written after Wharton had seen up close an actual war, no longer glorifies war as she had in earlier poems. In other poems it is the magic hour between daylight and dark that prompts visions of the sublime, while the final two poems offer the reader a deeper voyage into the center of the poet's creative genius.

In the winter of 1888, against their family's advice and risking their financial well-being, the newly married Whartons joined a friend on a four-month yacht tour of the Aegean Sea. They visited Sicily and saw Euryalus, the ruins of a fifth-century BCE Greek fortress near Syracuse, on the crest of the Epipolae ridge. In this early poem we can see Wharton's dramatic and historical imagination in bloom.

🐚 Euryalus

UPWARD we went by fields of asphodel,
Leaving Ortygia's moat-bound walls below;
By orchards, where the wind-flowers' drifted snow
Lay lightly heaped upon the turf's light swell;
By gardens, whence upon the wayside fell
Jasmine and rose in April's overflow,
Till, winding up Epipolae's wide brow,
We reached at last the lonely citadel.

There, on the ruined rampart climbing high,
We sat and dreamed among the browsing sheep,
Until we heard the trumpet's startled cry
Waking a clang of arms about the keep,
And seaward saw, with rapt, foreboding eye,
The sails of Athens whiten on the deep.

[1888] (1889)

Latomia dei Cappucini (Wharton's misspelling), the Quarry of the Capuchins, is in Syracuse. After their defeat in the Athens/Syracuse war in 413 BCE, seven thousand Athenian soldiers were imprisoned in the quarry and forced to work themselves to death. Later, Capuchin monks purchased the cave and created a magnificent garden that became a regular stop for those doing the "Grand Tour." Section I of the poem sets the scene, and it is written in trochaic octameter, the same rhythm as Poe's "The Raven" and Tennyson's "Locksley Hall." Section II, in a freer rhythm, is the voice of an Athenian warrior, trapped in the quarry, longing for home. The epigraph comes from John Wesley's commentary on Luke 11:32, on the fate of the Jews. We don't know when this poem was written—perhaps on that first Aegean cruise.

🐚 Latomia dei Cappucini
"They were destroyed with an utter destruction."

I

OVERHEAD the purple spaces of Sicilian twilight skies
Streaked with amber in long reaches, westward where the sunset
    dies;
Far below, in shadowy places, shapes of guardian cypresses,
And the surf still sighing on the beaches a long mournful cry
    from Salamis.

II

How the sun beats! There's not a breath to stir
Even overhead the fringe of grass that flickers

About the quarry's mouth; Each blade today
Is stencilled black against a sky of lapis.
O the cool breezes off Pentelicus!
O the sharp wind that churns to racing snow
The violet ripples of the sea at home!
How strange it is—I neither care today
For victory nor defeat, nor that keen shame
Which numbed all lesser pains—all these are one,
My soul has grown as slavish as my hands,
I have forgotten even the names of things
That used to thrill like wine—one longing only
Lives in me, and mine eyeballs burn with it;
To stand once more upon the shining steps
That from the city to the goddess lead,
Seeing below the roofs of those I love,
And, looking through the sun-smit colonnade,
That sky, so bluer than all bluest blues,
That overroofs our Athens—there to stand
And see the gleaming horsemen and the priests,
The youths and maidens in their bright-edged robes,
Familiar faces rapt with alien awe,
Unrecognizing as the statues' selves
They pass between, as the long column sweeps
On to the temple with a clash of song.
Oh to see this, to be a part of it,
Each pulse vibrating with the awful joy,
Each sense a-quiver with the light, the song,
The lambent laugh of colour everywhere!
Oh to be Athens, Athens to the soul,
One moment only—then to be no more.

Ah, how the sun's sword pierces thro' my brain,
And murders thought and memory—I might rest,
But see the quarry's edge bristles with blades,
Drawn blades of foes—or is it but the grass
Against the sky?———

Cleobis died last night.
He thought he lay upon his dear one's breast
And I, who held him, said no word to him.
Hark, how the lash falls! It comes nearer now—
Well, smite me then, and smite and smite and smite,
Till from its utmost citadel you drive
The last poor spark of life—and so well, done.
What? Have they passed me? What is this?
                              I stand
Free in the sunlight on the shining steps—
What song is this that swells upon the wind?
What lips, what arms, what flashing swords and shields?

Goddess! My Athens! . . . .

Cleobis, then I.—

[1889–93] (2019)

Segesta is a Greek temple, also in Sicily, which Wharton first saw with her dear friend and travel companion Walter Berry (1859–1927) in 1913, and again in 1926. Built between 430 and 420 BCE, the temple was never finished, having no roof or flutings on the columns. It is spectacularly large, measuring two hundred feet long and eighty-five feet wide. In a letter to their friend the art historian Bernard Berenson, she described the earlier visit: "We left Palermo two days ago, and went across those wonderful mountains behind Monreale to the Gaggera ford, where we lassoed two mettlesome mules and pranced up the sacred heights to the most inspired solitude on earth" (EW to BB, 19 April 1913, in Lewis and Lewis, *Letters of Edith Wharton* 296).

Segesta

HIGH in the secret places of the hills
Cliff-girt it stands, in grassy solitude,
No ruin but a vision unachieved.

This temple is a house not made with hands
But born of man's incorrigible need
For permanence and beauty in the scud
And wreckage of mortality—as though
Great thoughts, communing in the noise of towns
With inward isolation and deep peace,
And dreams gold-paven for celestial feet,
Had wrought the sudden wonder; and behold,
The sky, the hills, the awful colonnade,
And, night-long woven through the fane's august

Intercolumniations, all the stars
Processionally wheeling—

                    Then it was
That, having reared their wonder, it would seem
The makers feared their God might prove less great
Than man's heart dreaming on him—and so left
The shafts unroofed, untenanted the shrine.

[June 1926] (1926)

Beaulieu-sur-Mer sits on the Mediterranean Sea between Nice and Monaco. In ancient days it was the Greek port of Anao, later ruled by the Romans. Wharton knew the Riviera well, and she frequently picnicked along the coast. Here the speaker and a companion are at leisure, gazing at the sea, conjuring images of the glorious distant past. Wharton left two slightly different versions of this poem, one in her notebook and another in typescript, as if prepared for publication. I have used the typescript version, which seems to have been revised for repetition and cadence.

🐝 Beaulieu Wood

THE OLIVE and the ilex blend their boughs,
Light-shimmering silver shot with green austere,
In Beaulieu wood above our dreaming brows;
No voice of man, nor noise of life, is here,
But, far below, the sea's untrammelled blue,
Girdling the piny capes with fringe of snow,
Or purpling to the peacock's jewelled hue
In rock-bound inlets where no breezes blow
The selfsame sea whose waves erewhile have kissed
Carthage and Delos and the Lesbian height,
Whose sapphire currents, streaked with amethyst,
Have felt the Persian galleys' bleeding flight,
Or laughed about the joyous prows that bore
The flower of Athens to Sicilian graves;
Now, lapsing idly on this summer shore,
Those young, omniscient, sempiternal waves,
Heard of two idlers in the Beaulieu wood,
Murmur the story of their past again,

The throng of sails that lit their solitude,
The warfare and the triumph and the pain—
Two idlers amorous of the radiant past
And with the sullen present ill-content,
Who, in each vocal ripple shoreward cast,
Hear the faint echo of an old lament:—

"Lo, we have known the wonders of the world,
The pageant of its splendours have we known,
But now our fleets are gone, our sails are furled,
And wingèd memories sail on us alone.
Where are the magic prows that cleft our seas,
Where are the hollow ships by heroes manned,
Asail to find the fair Hesperides,
The purple phantom of some deathless land?
Then every valley stooping to our shore
Sheltered the foam-born nymph and nimble faun,
Each woodland hid the shepherd's honeyed store,
Brought to propitiate the gods at dawn;
The blue-haired sirens sang about our caves
In crystal shallows paved with bones of men,
And on the plumy summit of our waves
The laughing Nereids leapt and plunged again.
Then mighty cities, throned like queens, were fain
Their glorious image in our tides to glass,
And from their bastions leaning to the main
Watch the white pomp of navies pause and pass;
We bore their menaces from shore to shore,
Throbbing with messages of life or death,

And, part ourselves of the rash hearts we bore,
We leapt and panted with their warlike breath.

Now on our shores the grey decrepit towns
Shrunk in their walls in senile slumber lie,
With grassy streets where ghosts of old renowns
Walk lonely under the remembering sky.
Gone is the watchman from the crumbling tower,
Vanished in mist the last belated sail,
Like clouds that scatter with the sunset hour
Fled the last form of beauty and of bale,
Dead Sidon and dead Corinth, Carthage dead,
All the great queens whose feet we kissed of yore,
Fallen the crown from each dejected head,
Gone the last glory from our ancient shore."

[1889–93] (2019)

Here, writing in the 1890s, Wharton may have been observing a sunset from the porch of her Newport home, Land's End, which jutted into the sea. In the first stanza she imagines the coast as the scene of ancient Norse battles where Valkyrie accompany the heroic dead to their resting place. By the second stanza her imagination, still mythic, brings a more personal vision of mortality. One can see a Wordsworthian evocation of the sublime, but also perhaps the more sober observations on the ebbing Sea of Faith in Matthew Arnold's "Dover Beach."

🦋 An Autumn Sunset

I

LEAGUERED in fire
The wild black promontories of the coast extend
Their savage silhouettes;
The sun in universal carnage sets,
And, halting higher,
The motionless storm-clouds mass their sullen threats,
Like an advancing mob in sword-points penned,
That, balked, yet stands at bay.
Mid-zenith hangs the fascinated day
In wind-lustrated hollows crystalline,
A wan Valkyrie whose wide pinions shine
Across the ensanguined ruins of the fray,
And in her hand swings high o'erhead,
Above the waste of war,
The silver torch-light of the evening star
Wherewith to search the faces of the dead.

II

Lagooned in gold,
Seem not those jetty promontories rather
The outposts of some ancient land forlorn,
Uncomforted of morn,
Where old oblivions gather,
The melancholy unconsoling fold
Of all things that go utterly to death
And mix no more, no more
With life's perpetually awakening breath?
Shall Time not ferry me to such a shore,
Over such sailless seas,
To walk with hope's slain importunities
In miserable marriage? Nay, shall not
All things be there forgot,
Save the sea's golden barrier and the black
Close-crouching promontories?
Dead to all shames, forgotten of all glories,
Shall I not wander there, a shadow's shade,
A spectre self-destroyed,
So purged of all remembrance and sucked back
Into the primal void,
That should we on that shore phantasmal meet
I should not know the coming of your feet?

[1893?] (1894)

Another sunset poem, this one was written in 1907 or 1908 at Wharton's Massachusetts home, The Mount, where she had a view from her terrace of the Tyringham Hills. The speaker seems to see her own life in the death of day, followed by a new promise of moonlight and stars. Color, light, and darkness symbolize the essences of human experience.

Moonrise over Tyringham

Now the high holocaust of hours is done,
And all the west empurpled with their death,
How swift oblivion drinks the fallen sun,
How little while the dusk remembereth!

Though some there were, proud hours that marched in mail,
And took the morning on auspicious crest,
Crying to fortune "Back, for I prevail!"—
Yet now they lie disfeatured with the rest;

And some that stole so soft on destiny
Methought they had surprised her to a smile;
But these fled frozen when she turned to see,
And moaned and muttered through my heart awhile.

But now the day is emptied of them all,
And night absorbs their life-blood at a draught;
And so my life lies, as the gods let fall
An empty cup from which their lips have quaffed.

Yet see—night is not . . . by translucent ways,
Up the grey void of autumn afternoon
Steals a mild crescent, charioted in haze,
And all the air is merciful as June.

The lake is a forgotten streak of day
That trembles through the hemlocks' darkling bars,
And still, my heart, still some divine delay
Upon the threshold holds the earliest stars.

O pale equivocal hour, whose suppliant feet
Haunt the mute reaches of the sleeping wind,
Art thou a watcher stealing to entreat
Prayer and sepulture for thy fallen kind?

Poor plaintive waif of predestined race,
Their ruin gapes for thee. Why linger here?
Go hence in silence. Veil thine orphaned face,
Lest I should look on it and call it dear.

For if I love thee thou wilt sooner die;
Some sudden ruin will plunge upon thy head,
Midnight will fall from the revengeful sky
And hurl thee down among thy shuddering dead.

Avert thine eyes. Lapse softly from my sight,
Call not my name, nor heed if thine I crave,
So shalt thou sink through mitigated night
And bathe thee in the all-effacing wave.

But upward still thy perilous footsteps fare
Along a high-hung heaven drenched in light,
Dilating on a tide of crystal air
That floods the dark hills to their utmost height.

Strange hour, is this thy waning face that leans
Out of mid-heaven and makes my soul its glass?
What victory is imaged there? What means
Thy tarrying smile? Oh, veil thy lips and pass.

Nay . . . pause and let me name thee! For I see,
O with what flooding ecstasy of light,
Strange hour that wilt not loose thy hold on me,
Thou'rt not day's latest, but the first of night!

And after thee the gold-foot stars come thick,
From hand to hand they toss the flying fire,
Till all the zenith with their dance is quick
About the wheeling music of the Lyre.

Dread hour that lead'st the immemorial round,
With lifted torch revealing one by one
The thronging splendours that the day held bound,
And how each blue abyss enshrines its sun—

Be thou the image of a thought that fares
Forth from itself, and flings its ray ahead,
Leaping the barriers of ephemeral cares,
To where our lives are but the ages' tread,

And let this year be, not the last of youth,
But first—like thee!—of some new train of hours,
If more remote from hope, yet nearer truth,
And kin to the unpetitionable powers.

[1907–08] (1908)

Writing in 1915 after a half dozen tours of battlefields in France, Wharton dreamed of a healing landscape. The poem begins with an address to the sun, and once again it depicts a day going down to moonrise. This time, having seen real war, she evokes a cooling image meant to soothe the eyes of a war-weary soul.

🐛 Battle Sleep
[1915]

SOMEWHERE, O sun, some corner there must be
Thou visitest, where down the strand
Quietly, still, the waves go out to sea
From the green fringes of a pastoral land.

Deep in the orchard-bloom the roof-trees stand,
The brown sheep graze along the bay.
And through the apple-boughs above the sand
The bees' hum sounds no fainter than the spray.
There through uncounted hours declines the day
To the low arch of twilight's close,
And, just as night about the moon grows gray,
One sail leans westward to the fading rose.

Giver of dreams, O thou with scatheless wing
Forever moving through the fiery hail,
To flame-seared lids the cooling vision bring
And let some soul go seaward with that sail.

[1915] (1915)

Written when Wharton was sixty-one, this poem arises from the contem-
plation of the Mediterranean Sea from Hyères, on the French Riviera,
southwest of Cannes. As in "Moonrise over Tyringham," she is fascinated by
the transformation of day into night and all its possible symbolic meanings.
The "shapes that used to be / Part of the sunset" might be figures from
history and mythology, or perhaps more personal, intimate memories.

🐚 Les Salettes

LET all my waning senses reach
To clasp again that secret beach,
Pine-roofed and rock-embrasured, turned
To where the winter sunset burned
Beyond a purpling dolphin-cape
On charmèd seas asleep . . .
Let every murmur, every shape,
Fanned by that breathing hour's delight,
Against the widening western deep
Hold back the hour, hold back the night. . . .

For here, across the molten sea,
From golden islands lapped in gold,
Come all the shapes that used to be
Part of the sunset once to me,
And every breaker's emerald arch
Bears closer their ethereal march,
And flings its rose and lilac spray
To dress their brows with scattered day,

As trooping shoreward, one by one,
Swift in the pathway of the sun,
With lifted arms and eyes that greet,
The lost years hasten to my feet.

All is not pain, their eyes declare;
The shoreward ripples are their voice,
The sunset, streaming through their hair,
Coils round me in a fiery flood,
And all the sounds of that rich air
Are in the beating of my blood,
Crying: *Rejoice, rejoice, rejoice!*

Rejoice, because such skies are blue,
Each dawn, above a world so fair,
Because such glories still renew
To transient eyes the morning's hue,
Such buds on every fruit-tree smile,
Such perfumes blow on every gale,
Such constellated hangings veil
The outer emptiness awhile;
And these frail senses that were thine,
Because so frail, and worn so fine,
Are as a Venice glass, wherethrough
Life's last drop of evening wine
Shall like a draught of morning shine.

The glories go; their footsteps fade
Into an all-including shade,

And isles and sea and clouds and coasts
Wane to an underworld of ghosts.
But as I grope with doubtful foot
By myrtle branch and lentisk root
Up the precipitous pine-dark way,
Through fringes of the perished day
Falters a star, the first alight,
And threaded on that tenuous ray
The age-long promise reappears,
And life is Beauty, fringed with tears.

[December 1923] (1926)

This meditation on beauty was occasioned by Wharton's 1926 travel to Cyprus and Saint Hilarion Castle, called Dieu d'Amour by the French. The castle is enormous and perched high on top of a rocky mountain. Wharton's diary records: "3 hours in motor, an hour on donkey & foot. Very steep" (12 May 1926). She was sixty-four when she made this trip, still adventurous, still open to being captivated. As in the poem before, her style and diction are more relaxed, but her thoughts about Beauty are as lofty as ever.

🐛 Dieu d'Amour
[A Castle in Cyprus]

BEAUTY hath two great wings
That lift me to her height,
Though steep her secret dwelling clings
'Twixt earth and light.
Thither my startled soul she brings
In a murmur and stir of plumes,
And blue air cloven,
And in aerial rooms
Windowed on starry springs
Shows me the singing looms
Whereon her worlds are woven;

Then, in her awful breast,
Those heights descending,
Bears me, a child at rest,
At the day's ending,
Till earth, familiar as a nest,

Again receives me,
And Beauty veiled in night,
Benignly bending,
Drops from the sinking west
One feather of our flight,
And on faint sandals leaves me.

[May 16, 1926] (1926)

Wharton first published "La Folle du Logis" in 1910 under the name "The Comrade," and she liked it enough to include it in her 1926 volume, *Twelve Poems*. It's usually not a good idea to read the "I" of a poem as if it were the author, but in this case it seems almost inevitable. A tribute to her teeming imagination, "La Folle du Logis"—essentially the madwoman in the attic, from a French proverb, *"L'imagination est la folle du logis"*—invites us to see into the author's creative genius. It also links Wharton to numerous forebears, including the Brontë sisters, Christina Rossetti, Coleridge, Keats, and Wordsworth, all of whom described the worlds of their imagination. This astonishing evocation of her inner life reveals a Wharton never visible in her restrained prose or her corseted public figure.

La Folle du Logis

WILD wingèd thing, O brought I know not whence
To beat your life out in my life's low cage;
You strange familiar, nearer than my flesh
Yet distant as a star, that were at first
A child with me a child, yet elfin-far,
And visibly of some unearthly breed;
Mirthfullest mate of all my mortal games,
Yet shedding on them some evasive gleam
Of Latmian loneliness—O even then
Expert to lift the latch of our low door
And profit by the hours when, dusked about
By human misintelligence, we made
Our first weak fledgling flights—
Divine accomplice of those perilous-sweet
Low moth-flights of the unadventured soul

Above the world's dim garden!—now we sit
After what stretch of years, what stretch of wings,
In the same cage together—still as near
And still as strange!
                              Only I know at last
That we are fellows till the last night falls,
And that I shall not miss your comrade hands
Till they have closed my lids, and by them set
A taper that—who knows?—may yet shine through.

Sister, my comrade, I have ached for you,
Sometimes, to see you curb your pace to mine,
And bow your Maenad crest to the dull forms
Of human usage; I have loosed your hand
And whispered: "Go! Since I am tethered here";
And you have turned, and breathing for reply:
"I too am pinioned, as you too are free,"
Have caught me to such undreamed distances
As the last planets see, when they look forth
To the sentinel pacings of the outmost stars—
Nor these alone,
Comrade, my sister, were your gifts. More oft
Has your impalpable wing-brush bared for me
The heart of wonder in familiar things,
Unroofed dull rooms, and hung above my head
The cloudy glimpses of a vernal moon,
Or all the autumn heaven ripe with stars.

And you have made a secret pact with Sleep,
And when she comes not, or her feet delay,

Toiled in low meadows of gray asphodel
Under a pale sky where no shadows fall,
Then, hooded like her, to my side you steal,
And the night grows like a great rumouring sea,
And you a boat, and I your passenger,
And the tide lifts us with an indrawn breath
Out, out upon the murmurs and the scents,
Through spray of splintered star-beams, or white rage
Of desperate moon-drawn waters—on and on
To some blue sea's unalterable calm
That ever like a slow-swung mirror rocks
The balanced breasts of sea-birds. . . .

Yet other nights, my sister, you have been
The storm, and I the leaf that fled on it
Terrifically down voids that never knew
The pity of creation—till your touch
Has drawn me back to earth, as, in the dusk,
A scent of lilac from an unseen hedge
Bespeaks the hidden farm, the bedded cows,
And safety, and the sense of human kind. . . .

And I have climbed with you by secret ways
To meet the dews of morning, and have seen
The shy gods like retreating shadows fade,
Or on the thymy reaches have surprised
Old Chiron sleeping, and have waked him not . . .

Yet farther have I fared with you, and known
Love and his sacred tremors, and the rites

Of his most inward temple; and beyond
Have seen the long gray waste where lonely thoughts
Listen and wander where a city stood.

And creeping down by waterless defiles
Under an iron midnight, have I kept
My vigil in the waste till dawn began
To walk among the ruins, and I saw
A sapling rooted in a fissured plinth,
And a wren's nest in the thunder-threatening hand
Of some old god of granite. . . .

[1909–10] (1910)

As with "La Folle du Logis" (although other readings are possible), one can read this strange, deeply Romantic poem as an allegory exploring the sources of poetic creation. The speaker is a reed, plucked by Life, fashioned into a flute, and carried off on a wild journey that brings forth song. The initial idea may have come from Sonnet VII of *A Book of Day-Dreams* by Charles Leonard Moore, whose work she admired because it was "packed with imagination" (EW to Anna Bahlmann, 9 January 1893, Goldman-Price, *My Dear Governess* 105). Moore's words were "Man in Life's stream is like a shaken reed,— / Silent for all the river's mouthing it." Wharton's reed is far from silent. Contemporary critics praised this poem highly: *The Nation* in London called it a "magnificent rhapsody."

Life

NAY, lift me to thy lips, Life, and once more
Pour the wild music through me—

    I quivered in the reed-bed with my kind,
Rooted in Lethe-bank, when at the dawn
There came a groping shape of mystery
Moving among us, that with random stroke
Severed, and rapt me from my silent tribe,
Pierced, fashioned, lipped me, sounding for a voice,
Laughing on Lethe-bank—and in my throat
I felt the wing-beat of the fledgeling notes,
The bubble of godlike laughter in my throat.

Such little songs she sang,
Pursing her lips to fit the tiny pipe,

They trickled from me like a slender spring
That strings frail wood-growths on its crystal thread,
Nor dreams of glassing cities, bearing ships.
She sang, and bore me through the April world
Matching the birds, doubling the insect-hum
In the meadows, under the low-moving airs,
And breathings of the scarce-articulate air
When it makes mouths of grasses—but when the sky
Burst into storm, and took great trees for pipes,
She thrust me in her breast, and warm beneath
Her cloudy vesture, on her terrible heart,
I shook, and heard the battle.

　　　　　　But more oft,
Those early days, we moved in charmèd woods,
Where once, at dusk, she piped against a faun,
And one warm dawn a tree became a nymph
Listening; and trembled; and Life laughed and passed.
And once we came to a great stream that bore
The stars upon its bosom like a sea,
And ships like stars; so to the sea we came.
And there she raised me to her lips, and sent
One swift pang through me; then refrained her hand,
And whispered: "Hear—" and into my frail flanks,
Into my bursting veins, the whole sea poured
Its spaces and its thunder; and I feared.

We came to cities, and Life piped on me
Low calls to dreaming girls,
In counting-house windows, through the chink of gold,

Flung cries that fired the captive brain of youth,
And made the heavy merchant at his desk
Curse us for a cracked hurdy-gurdy; Life
Mimicked the hurdy-gurdy, and we passed.

We climbed the slopes of solitude, and there
Life met a god, who challenged her and said:
"Thy pipe against my lyre!" But "Wait!" she laughed,
And in my live flank dug a finger-hole,
And wrung new music from it. Ah, the pain!

We climbed and climbed, and left the god behind.
We saw the earth spread vaster than the sea,
With infinite surge of mountains surfed with snow,
And a silence that was louder than the deep;
But on the utmost pinnacle Life again
Hid me, and I heard the terror in her hair.

Safe in new vales, I ached for the old pang,
And clamoured "Play me against a god again!"
"Poor Marsyas-mortal—he shall bleed thee yet,"
She breathed and kissed me, stilling the dim need.
But evermore it woke, and stabbed my flank
With yearnings for new music and new pain.
"Another note against another god!"
I clamoured; and she answered: "Bide my time.
Of every heart-wound I will make a stop,
And drink thy life in music, pang by pang.
But first thou must yield the notes I stored in thee
At dawn beside the river. Take my lips."

She kissed me like a lover, but I wept,
Remembering that high song against the god,
And the old songs slept in me, and I was dumb.

We came to cavernous foul places, blind
With harpy-wings, and sulphurous with the glare
Of sinful furnaces—where hunger toiled,
And pleasure gathered in a starveling prey,
And death fed delicately on young bones.

"Now sing!" cried Life, and set her lips to me.
"Here are gods also. Wilt thou pipe for Dis?"
My cry was drowned beneath the furnace roar,
Choked by the sulphur-fumes; and beast-lipped gods
Laughed down on me, and mouthed the flutes of hell.

"Now sing!" said Life, reissuing to the stars;
And wrung a new note from my wounded side.

So came we to clear spaces, and the sea.
And now I felt its volume in my heart,
And my heart waxed with it, and Life played on me
The song of the Infinite. "Now the stars," she said.

Then from the utmost pinnacle again
She poured me on the wild sidereal stream,
And I grew with her great breathings, till we swept
The interstellar spaces like new worlds
Loosed from the fiery ruin of a star.

Cold, cold we rested on black peaks again,
Under black skies, under a groping wind;
And Life, grown old, hugged me to a numb breast,
Pressing numb lips against me. Suddenly
A blade of silver severed the black peaks
From the black sky, and earth was born again,
Breathing and various, under a god's feet.
A god! A god! I felt the heart of Life
Leap under me, and my cold flanks shook again.
He bore no lyre, he rang no challenge out,
But Life warmed to him, warming me with her,
And as he neared I felt beneath her hands
The stab of a new wound that sucked my soul
Forth in a new song from my throbbing throat.

"His name—his name?" I whispered, but she shed
The music faster, and I grew with it,
Became a part of it, while Life and I
Clung lip to lip, and I from her wrung song
As she from me, one song, one ecstasy,
In indistinguishable union blent,
Till she became the flute and I the player.
And lo! the song I played on her was more
Than any she had drawn from me; it held
The stars, the peaks, the cities, and the sea,
The faun's catch, the nymph's tremor, and the heart
Of dreaming girls, of toilers at the desk,
Apollo's challenge on the sunrise slope,
And the hiss of the night-gods mouthing flutes of hell—
All, to the dawn-wind's whisper in the reeds,

When Life first came, a shape of mystery,
Moving among us, and with random stroke
Severed, and rapt me from my silent tribe.
All this I wrung from her in that deep hour,
While Love stood murmuring: "Play the god, poor grass!"

Now, by that hour, I am a mate to thee
Forever, Life, however spent and clogged,
And tossed back useless to my native mud!
Yea, groping for new reeds to fashion thee
New instruments of anguish and delight,
Thy hand shall leap to me, thy broken reed,
Thine ear remember me, thy bosom thrill
With the old subjection, then when Love and I
Held thee, and fashioned thee, and made thee dance
Like a slave-girl to her pipers—yea, thou yet
Shalt hear my call, and dropping all thy toys
Thou'lt lift me to thy lips, Life, and once more
Pour the wild music through me—

[1892–1908?] (1908)

A Public Voice

Moving from the inner world to the outer, we encounter a completely different kind of poetry. Throughout her life, Wharton wrote occasional poems to call attention to injustice and heroism, to celebrate public events, and to eulogize friends who gave their lives in noble causes. Two-thirds of the poems presented here were written between 1914 and 1919, the years of World War I. Wharton, living in Paris, was deeply engaged in organizing relief work, providing jobs for unemployed women and housing for children, refugees, and people with tuberculosis. She organized and published a gift book called *The Book of the Homeless*, for which she solicited poems, stories, drawings, and even musical compositions from noted artists. She herself wrote a poem ("The Tryst") and translated all the materials sent to her in other languages. Proceeds from the sale of the book went to fund her charities. Wharton also made several trips to the front with her friend Walter Berry to bring supplies and report on the war for *Scribner's Magazine*.

The first poems in this section were written much earlier, when she was a girl and young woman, demonstrating that even as a child she read the newspaper and cared about injustice and poverty. Wharton was not a believer in woman suffrage, but she did believe that people had an obligation to help others. These poems reflect her moral vision of public responsibility and service.

"Only a Child" is the first-known publicly published poem by Edith Wharton, then Edith Jones, written when she was seventeen and appearing in the *New York World*. She wrote it in response to a newspaper story about a little boy imprisoned in the House of Refuge in Philadelphia, an institution founded by Quakers in the 1820s for the care of delinquent and vagrant children. The boy killed himself while under solitary confinement. Rather than give her proper name, Wharton signed herself "Eadgyth," after the Queen Consort of Germany, granddaughter of Alfred the Great, wife of Holy Roman Emperor Otto I (910–946 CE). Here was a young poet with a good grounding in history and myth, a sympathetic imagination, a public conscience, and great ambition.

🐦 Only a Child

THEY found him hanging dead, you know,
    In the cell where he had lain
Through many a day of restless woe
    And night of sleepless pain.
The heart had ceased its beating,
    The little hands were numb,
And the piteous voice entreating
    In death at last was dumb.

No doubt it was a painful fact
    For them to contemplate;
They felt the horror of the act,
    But felt it rather late.
There was none to lay the blame to—
    That, each one understands;

And the jury found—he came to
    His death by his own hands!

Poor little hands! that should have known
    No subtler arts than these—
To seek for violets newly blown
    Beneath the April breeze,
Or gaily bind unchidden
    The daisies into sheaves,
Or reach the bird's nest hidden
    Among the budding leaves.

Poor little hands! And little heart
    That ached so long alone,
With none to ease its secret smart
    And none to hear its moan;
As he lay where they had cast him
    In the dark upon the floor,
And heard the feet go past him
    Outside his prison door.

Think of him, you whose children lie
    Soft sleeping overhead;
All day he could not see the sky,
    All night he had no bed.
Four walls of brick and mortar
    To shut the child's soul in,
And starving on bread and water
    For—some little childish sin!

So in the darkness there he lay
    While the hours crawled along,
And thought of the woodlands far away
    Awake with the robin's song;
And thought of the green grass growing
    And the boys at play outside,
And the breath of heaven blowing
    O'er the country far and wide.

Perhaps he saw his mother's face
    Bend o'er him in the gloom;
But when he leaned to catch her dress
    She vanished from the room;
And though he tried to remember
    The prayer he used to say,
In a pitiful, broken stammer
    On his lips it died away.

His little hands had nought to do
    But beat against the wall,
Until at last too tired they grew—
    Poor little hands—so small!
And so he lay there voiceless,
    Alone upon the ground;
If he wept, his tears were noiseless,
    For he feared to hear their sound.

At last perhaps the silence grew
    Too deep—it dazed his head—

And his little hands had naught to do;
    And so—they found him dead!
In a Christian town it happened,
    In a home for children built,
And God knows whose soul shall answer
    For the burden of this guilt!

But He who bade the children come
    And not be turned away,
Has surely taken the homeless home,
    And we need not mourn to-day;
For our lives are all God-given,
    The poorest to Him is dear,
And the Father has room in heaven
    For the children we don't want here!

[May 1879] (1879)

As she had with "Only a Child," Wharton published this occasional poem in the *New York World* under the pseudonym Eadgyth. The second USS *Constellation*, commissioned in 1855, was a warship used in the Civil War and later as a naval training ship. Refitted specially for the purpose, from March to June 1880, she carried relief supplies to a famished Ireland. It is interesting to see the eighteen-year-old's dualistic view of war and battle, an attitude she would carry into World War I until she grew weary and sick of the carnage and chaos.

The Constellation's Last Victory
[FOR THE WORLD]

NOT armed for devastation,
   Nor manned to meet the fray,
The old ship Constellation
   Has set her sails to-day.
She has seen the flames of battle leap,
   And now that warfares cease,
She wings her way across the deep,
   A messenger of peace.

A name of consolation
   In realms across the sea
Shall the warlike Constellation
   Henceforth forever be;
A strong-winged Angel of the Lord
   With gifts of wine and bread,
She hastes to crown the starving board
   'Mid the dying and the dead.

And, as for their salvation,
     Men yearn and wait and weep
To see the Constellation
     Arise upon the deep—
The shores shall not be manned to meet
     Her cannon's angry stare,
But every door set wide to greet
     An angel unaware.

With plenty for starvation,
     With strength for the opprest,
The good ship Constellation
     The fiercest storm shall breast,
And she whom foemen dreaded sore
     Of old on many seas
In age shall win one victory more,
     The victory of peace.

[March 28, 1880] (1880)

We cannot know when this unpublished poem was written, but the concerns of the poem, and the intriguing use of the name "Edith" for the character who unwittingly initiates the action of the poem, suggest perhaps a young author contemplating the implications of her life, as she would do more fully in *The House of Mirth*. Her understanding that even the neediest people crave beauty as well as food reveals much about her own love of beauty; the poem almost certainly predates the political slogan "bread and roses."

The Rose

THE ROSE that fell last night from Edith's hair
In coming from the ball, lay flushed and torn
On the wet sidewalk in the bitter air
Till suddenly a draggled shape forlorn,
With shabby shawl and drenched uncovered head,
Sprang through the carriages and snatched it up.
The footmen laughed, but she, with painful red
Scorching her haggard cheekbones, through the group
Fled to the darkness of a lonelier street.
Still hastening on, for haunts of drabs and thieves
She left the lamplit highway, till her feet
Found the familiar stairway to the eaves
Of a bleak tenement that sobbed with rain.
She pushed a door, and entered in. The room
Was dark, and through a broken window-pane
Clamoured the dripping wind. In the cold gloom

Her children crouched. The eldest struck a light,
And by the glimmering tallow she could see   .
Three little starving faces clustered, white
As ghosts of happier children, at her knee.

"What have you brought us, Mother? Hush, I know
There's something in her shawl!"
                            The mother smiled
And, leaning down to the faint candle-glow,
Held out the rose-bud to her hungry child.

"Mother, what's that? And is it good to eat?"
They cried together.
                            "No, not that" she said.
"It's only a rose, dears, but it smells so sweet!
Around my father's doorway, overhead,
They grew by hundreds, rank as weeds, in June,
And sweeter far than this. On Summer eves
We used to sit and watch the friendly moon
Peer like a neighbour's face between their leaves,
And when my father drove us to the fair
(Where there was dancing in a big white tent)
I always wore a red rose in my hair,
And a gold brooch of mother's"—
                            With intent
Wide gaze upon her dreaming face they stood,
While on the rose her tears like raindrops rolled,
And they were quiet, trying to be good,
Though they were starving and the night was cold,
But when at length she lifted up her head

One of them said, with grave rebuking eye,
"Mother, you promised us a loaf of bread"—

And then the youngest one began to cry.

[1889–93] (2019)

Along with her elegy for Theodore Roosevelt ("With the Tide"), "A Torch-bearer" was one of the most widely reproduced of Wharton's poems during her lifetime. It is an elegy for James Brown Markoe (1865–1902), a young man from a prominent family who was an acquaintance of the Whartons. He died on the way to the theater with three friends, in a carriage accident during which his brave intervention saved the lives of the other passengers. The poem appeared in *Scribner's Magazine*, then in *Literary Digest*, in the twenty-fifth-anniversary volume of Markoe's class at Harvard, and it was picked up by numerous local newspapers and magazines. Lines and sections from the poem appeared later in collections of sermons and volumes published by patriotic societies. One interesting appearance was in the Annual Proceedings of the Sons of the Revolution, Pennsylvania Society, where the lines are applied to George Washington. Clearly Wharton's words resonated for many readers.

A Torchbearer
(J. B. M. November 29, 1902)

GREAT cities rise and have their fall; the brass
That held their glories moulders in its turn,
Hard granite rots like an uprooted weed,
And ever on the palimpsest of earth
Impatient Time rubs out the word he writ.
But one thing makes the years its pedestal,
Springs from the ashes of its pyre, and claps
A skyward wing above its epitaph—
The will of man willing immortal things.

The ages are but baubles hung upon
The thread of some strong lives—and one slight wrist
May lift a century above the dust;
For Time,
The Sisyphean load of little lives,
Becomes the globe and sceptre of the great.
But who are these that, linking hand in hand,
Transmit across the twilight waste of years
The flying brightness of a kindled hour?
Not always, nor alone, the lives that search
How they may snatch a glory out of heaven
Or add a height to Babel; oftener they
That in the still fulfilment of each day's
Pacific order hold great deeds in leash,
That in the sober sheath of tranquil tasks
Hide the attempered blade of high emprise,
And leap like lightning to the clap of fate.

So greatly gave he, nurturing 'gainst the call
Of one rare moment all the daily store
Of joy distilled from the acquitted task,
And that deliberate rashness which bespeaks
The pondered action passed into the blood;
So swift to harden purpose into deed
That, with the wind of ruin in his hair,
Soul sprang full-statured from the broken flesh,
And at one stroke he lived the whole of life,
Poured all in one libation to the truth,
A brimming flood whose drops shall overflow
On deserts of the soul long beaten down

By the brute hoof of habit, till they spring
In manifold upheaval to the sun.

Call here no high artificer to raise
His wordy monument—such lives as these
Make death a dull misnomer and its pomp
An empty vesture. Let resounding lives
Re-echo splendidly through high-piled vaults
And make the grave their spokesman—such as he
Are as the hidden streams that, underground,
Sweeten the pastures for the grazing kine,
Or as spring airs that bring through prison bars
The scent of freedom; or a light that burns
Immutably across the shaken seas,
Forevermore by nameless hands renewed,
Where else were darkness and a glutted shore.

[1902] (1903)

"High Pasture" celebrates the life of the teacher, scholar, and editor Charles Eliot Norton (1827–1908), a friend and mentor to Wharton. Included in a collection of tributes to Norton for his eightieth birthday, the poem commemorates a life of the mind, well lived. Norton's house in Ashfield, Massachusetts, sits at the bottom of a hill, with a high pasture just across the way.

High Pasture

(Ashfield, November 6, 1907)

COME up—come up: in the dim vale below
The autumn mist muffles the fading trees,
But on this keen hill-pasture, though the breeze
Has stretched the thwart boughs bare to meet the snow,
Night is not, autumn is not—but the flow
Of vast, ethereal and irradiate seas,
Poured from the far world's flaming boundaries
In waxing tides of unimagined glow.

And to that height illumined of the mind
He calls us still by the familiar way,
Leaving the sodden tracks of life behind,
Befogged in failure, chilled with love's decay—
Showing us, as the night-mists upward wind,
How on the heights is day and still more day.

[Lenox 1907] (1908)

People often assume that Wharton wrote only about the world of wealth and high society, but, like "The Rose" and her earlier story "Bunner Sisters," this 1902 poem reminds us that she was well aware of the underside of that life of privilege and waste. The speaker is one of Wharton's *flaneurs*, an idle gentleman who walks the city simply to observe and reflect on what he sees.

The Bread of Angels

AT that lost hour disowned of day and night,
The after-birth of midnight, when life's face
Turns to the wall and the last lamp goes out
Before the incipient irony of dawn—
In that obliterate interval of time
Between the oil's last flicker and the first
Reluctant shudder of averted day,
Threading the city's streets (like mine own ghost
Wakening the echoes of dispeopled dreams),
I smiled to see how the last light that fought
Extinction was the old familiar glare
Of supper tables under gas-lit ceilings,
The same old stale monotonous carouse
Of greed and surfeit nodding face to face
O'er the picked bones of pleasure . . .
So that the city seemed, at that waste hour,
Like some expiring planet from whose face
All nobler life had perished—love and hate,
And labor and the ecstasy of thought—
Leaving the eyeless creatures of the ooze,

Dull offspring of its first inchoate birth,
The last to cling to its exhausted breast.

And threading thus the aimless streets that strayed
Conjectural through a labyrinth of death,
Strangely I came upon two hooded nuns,
Hands in their sleeves, heads bent as if beneath
Some weight of benediction, gliding by
Punctual as shadows that perform their round
Upon the inveterate bidding of the sun.
Again and yet again their ordered course
At the same hour crossed mine: obedient shades
Cast by some high-orbed pity on the waste
Of midnight evil! and my wondering thoughts
Tracked them from the hushed convent where their kin
Lay hived in sweetness of their prayer-built cells.
What wind of fate had loosed them from the lee
Of that dear anchorage where their sisters slept?
On what emprise of heavenly piracy
Did such frail craft put forth upon this world;
In what incalculable currents caught
And swept beyond the signal-lights of home
Did their white coifs set sail against the night?

At last, upon my wonder drawn, I followed
The secret wanderers till I saw them pause
Before the dying glare of those tall panes
Where greed and surfeit nodded face to face
O'er the picked bones of pleasure . . .
And the door opened and the nuns went in.

Again I met them, followed them again.
Straight as a thought of mercy to its goal
To the same door they sped. I stood alone.
And suddenly the silent city shook
With inarticulate clamor of gagged lips,
As in Jerusalem when the veil was rent
And the dead drove the living from the streets.
And all about me stalked the shrouded dead,
Dead hopes, dead efforts, loves and sorrows dead,
With empty orbits groping for their dead
In that blind mustering of murdered faiths . . .
And the door opened and the nuns came out.

I turned and followed. Once again we came
To such a threshold, such a door received them,
They vanished, and I waited. The grim round
Ceased only when the festal panes grew dark
And the last door had shot its tardy bolt.
"Too late!" I heard one murmur; and "Too late!"
The other, in unholy antiphon.
And with dejected steps they turned away.

They turned, and still I tracked them, till they bent
Under the lee of a calm convent wall
Bounding a quiet street. I knew the street,
One of those village byways strangely trapped
In the city's meshes, where at loudest noon
The silence spreads like moss beneath the foot,
And all the tumult of the town becomes
Idle as Ocean's fury in a shell.

Silent at noon—but now, at this void hour,
When the blank sky hung over the blank streets
Clear as a mirror held above dead lips,
Came footfalls, and a thronging of dim shapes
About the convent door: a suppliant line
Of pallid figures, ghosts of happier folk,
Moving in some gray underworld of want
On which the sun of plenty never dawns.
And as the nuns approached I saw the throng,
Pale emanation of that outcast hour,
Divide like vapor when the sun breaks through
And take the glory on its tattered edge.
For so a brightness ran from face to face,
Faint as a diver's light beneath the sea,
And as a wave draws up the beach, the crowd
Drew to the nuns.
                    I waited. Then those two
Strange pilgrims of the sanctuaries of sin
Brought from beneath their large conniving cloaks
Two hidden baskets brimming with rich store
Of broken viands—pasties, jellies, meats,
Crumbs of Belshazzar's table, evil waste
Of that interminable nightly feast
Of greed and surfeit, nodding face to face
O'er the picked bones of pleasure . . .
And piteous hands were stretched to take the bread
Of this strange sacrament—this manna brought
Out of the antique wilderness of sin.

Each seized a portion, turning comforted
From this new breaking of the elements;
And while I watched the mystery of renewal
Whereby the dead bones of old sins became
The living body of the love of God,
It seemed to me that a like change transformed
The city's self . . . a little wandering air
Ruffled the ivy on the convent wall;
A bird piped doubtfully; the dawn replied;
And in that ancient gray necropolis
Somewhere a child awoke and took the breast.

[?] (1902)

In August 1915, one year into the Great War, Wharton published this poem in the *New York Times*. Reminding readers of the American Revolution and what it meant, the poem expresses her strongly held conviction that the United States had a responsibility to help defend France—and civilization—by joining in the war. The Palace of Peace, invoked in the penultimate stanza, was a building in The Hague built with international cooperation and funds from Andrew Carnegie and finished in 1913, a year before the war. Presently it houses several judicial institutions; when the poem was written, it was the home of the international Permanent Court of Arbitration. From this poem, which was reprinted many times in the first years of the war, may come the phrase made famous by Herman Wouk, "the winds of war."

The Great Blue Tent

COME unto me, said the Flag,
Ye weary and sore opprest;
For I am no shot-riddled rag,
But a great blue tent of rest.

Ye heavy laden, come
On the aching feet of dread,
From ravaged town, from murdered home,
From your tortured and your dead.

All they that beat at my crimson bars
Shall enter without demur.
Though the round earth rock with the wind of wars,
Not one of my folds shall stir.

See, here is warmth and sleep,
And a table largely spread.
I give garments to them that weep,
And for gravestones I give bread.

But what, through my inmost fold,
Is this cry on the winds of war?
Are you grown so old, are you grown so cold,
O Flag that was once our star?

Where did you learn that bread is life,
And where that fire is warm—
You, that took the van of a world-wide strife,
As an eagle takes the storm?

Where did you learn that men are bred
Where hucksters bargain and gorge;
And where that down makes a softer bed
Than the snows of Valley Forge?

Come up, come up to the stormy sky,
Where our fierce folds rattle and hum,
For Lexington taught us how to fly,
And we dance to Concord's drum.

O flags of freedom, said the Flag,
Brothers of wind and sky;
I too was once a tattered rag,
And I wake and shake at your cry.

I tug and tug at the anchoring place,
Where my drowsy folds are caught;
I strain to be off on the old fierce chase
Of the foe we have always fought.

O People I made, said the Flag,
And welded from sea to sea,
I am still the shot-riddled rag,
That shrieks to be free, to be free.

Oh, cut my silken ties
From the roof of the palace of peace;
Give back my stars to the skies,
My stripes to the storm-striped seas!

Or else, if you bid me yield,
Then down with my crimson bars.
And o'er all my azure field
Sow poppies instead of stars.

[1915] (1915)

King Albert's Book: A Tribute to the Belgian King and People from Representative Men and Women Throughout the World, jointly published by several newspapers, was a gift book produced for Christmas sale in 1914. Proceeds benefitted the Daily Telegraph Belgian Fund. The epigraph for Wharton's contribution, translated as "Belgium regrets nothing," is a quotation from the Belgian prime minister, Charles Baron de Broqueville.

Belgium

La Belgique ne regrette rien.

NOT with her ruined silver spires,
Not with her cities shamed and rent,
Perish the imperishable fires
That shape the homestead from the tent.

Wherever men are staunch and free,
There shall she keep her fearless state,
And, homeless, to great nations be
The home of all that makes them great.

[1914] (1914)

Having seen the destruction of war up close and meeting some of the refugees from Belgium, Wharton had enormous respect for their stoic endurance and unshaken love of country. She wrote this poem to include in *The Book of the Homeless*. Some critics have argued that her war poetry is overly sentimental and out of step with other, more disillusioned and bitter war writings by people like Wilfred Owen and Ernest Hemingway.

The Tryst

I SAID to the woman: Whence do you come,
With your bundle in your hand?
She said: In the North I made my home,
Where slow streams fatten the fruitful loam,
And the endless wheat-fields run like foam
To the edge of the endless sand.

I said: What look have your houses there,
And the rivers that glass your sky?
Do the steeples that call your people to prayer
Lift fretted fronts to the silver air,
And the stones of your streets, are they washed and fair
When the Sunday folk go by?

My house is ill to find, she said,
For it has no roof but the sky;
The tongue is torn from the steeple-head,
The streets are foul with the slime of the dead,
And all the rivers run poison-red
With the bodies drifting by.

I said: Is there none to come at your call
In all this throng astray?
They shot my husband against a wall,
And my child (she said), too little to crawl,
Held up its hands to catch the ball
When the gun-muzzle turned its way.

I said: There are countries far from here
Where the friendly church-bells call,
And fields where the rivers run cool and clear,
And streets where the weary may walk without fear,
And a quiet bed, with a green tree near,
To sleep at the end of it all.

She answered: Your land is too remote,
And what if I chanced to roam
When the bells fly back to the steeples' throat,
And the sky with banners is all afloat,
And the streets of my city rock like a boat
With the tramp of her men come home?

I shall crouch by the door till the bolt is down,
And then go in to my dead.
Where my husband fell I will put a stone,
And mother a child instead of my own,
And stand and laugh on my bare hearth-stone
When the King rides by, she said.

[Paris, August 27, 1915]' (1916)

The war brought death to many of Wharton's friends and sons of friends. One of these was the soldier, explorer, and writer Jean du Breuil de Saint-Germain (1873–1915), a member of the salon society that Wharton enjoyed. They knew each other well, and du Breuil was engaged to be married to a friend of Wharton's when he was killed in action.

Beaumetz, February 23rd. 1915.
(Jean du Breuil de St. Germain)

So much of life was sudden thrust
Under this dumb disfiguring dust,
Such laughter, hopes, impatient power,
Such visions of a rounded hour,
Such ardour for things deep and great,
Such easy disregard of fate,
Such memories of strange lands remote,
Of solitudes where eagles float,
Of plains where under other stars
Strange races lock in alien wars,
And isles of spicery that sleep
Unroused on an unfurrowed deep—

All this—and then his voice, his eyes,
His eager questions, gay replies,
The warmth he put into the air—
And, oh, his step upon the stair!
Poor grave, too narrow to contain
Such store of life, in vain, in vain,
The grass-roots and the ivy-ropes

Shall pinion all those springing hopes,
In vain the ivy and the grass
Efface the sense of what he was,
Poor grave!—for he shall burst your ties,
And come to us with shining eyes,
And laughter, and a quiet jest,
Whenever we, who loved him best,
Speak of great actions simply done,
And lives not vain beneath the sun.

[Easter 1915] (2004)

Here we have another elegy, this time for Ronald Simmons (c. 1887–1918), a young American who came to Paris to study architecture and was befriended by Wharton. During the war, he served as secretary to one of her charities, and when the United States entered the war he volunteered for the American Expeditionary Forces and signed on as a captain in intelligence. He died in Marseilles, where he was stationed, of pneumonia. Wharton was very fond of him and deeply affected by his death; later she modeled her character Boylston, in *A Son at the Front*, partly on Simmons.

"On Active Service"
AMERICAN EXPEDITIONARY FORCE
(R.S., August 12th, 1918)

HE is dead that was alive.
How shall friendship understand?
Lavish heart and tireless hand
Bidden not to give or strive,
Eager brain and questing eye
Like a broken lens laid by.

He, with so much left to do,
Such a gallant race to run,
What concern had he with you,
Silent Keeper of things done?

Tell us not that, wise and young,
Elsewhere he lives out his plan.
Our speech was sweetest to his tongue,
And his great gift was to be man.

Long and long shall we remember,
In our breasts his grave be made.
It shall never be December
Where so warm a heart is laid,
But in our saddest selves a sweet voice sing,
Recalling him, and Spring.

[1918] (1918)

Wharton was enormously proud of the young Americans who came to Europe to offer their strength and good nature, their bodies and their lives, in what she considered the fight for Western civilization. She wrote this poem in 1919 for a newsletter published by the Red Cross in an American encampment for soldiers located near her home in Hyères, France. The soldiers—who had served bravely, some wounded—were shortly to ship out for home. Notice how she writes, not in her usual language of high poetry, but in the vernacular spoken by the young Americans, and notice also her dual allegiance to America and France.

Farewell to France

BEFORE we go back to the land that's our own
Here's a thought for the land we're leaving.
A thought of kindness for kindness done,
And of pity for lone hearts grieving.

There may have been friction now and again,
As happens when two go shares—
It's a pity they don't talk our language—but then
How is it *we* don't talk theirs?

There've been times when, if things were not done our way,
We were sure they were not worth a glance;
But once we're at home will not some of us say:
"You should see how they do *that* in France?"

Remember it now—no two lands are alike;
But, though heavy the differences weigh,

How light they will seem when we see the dawn strike
The Liberty who waits up the bay!

And when we behold her, new born to the sky,
Her torch lifted up like a lance,
Be sure she will breathe, as the transports go by:
"My light was first kindled in France!"

[1919] (1919)

Here is another poem addressed to the soldiers, this one written just days after the armistice ending the war was signed. It has been read both as a glorification of war and as a deep expression of sadness and gratitude for the young Americans whose lives were interrupted, some lost, for a cause that did not directly affect them.

You and You

TO THE AMERICAN PRIVATE IN THE GREAT WAR

EVERY one of you won the war—
You and you and you—
Each one knowing what it was for,
And what was his job to do.

Every one of you won the war,
Obedient, unwearied, unknown,
Dung in the trenches, drift on the shore,
Dust to the world's end blown;
Every one of you, steady and true,
You and you and you—
Down in the pit or up in the blue,
Whether you crawled or sailed or flew,
Whether your closest comrade knew
Or you bore the brunt alone—

All of you, all of you, name after name,
Jones and Robinson, Smith and Brown,
You from the piping prairie town,
You from the Fundy fogs that came,

You from the city's roaring blocks,
You from the bleak New England rocks
With the shingled roof in the apple boughs,
You from the brown adobe house—
You from the Rockies, you from the Coast,
You from the burning frontier-post
And you from the Klondyke's frozen flanks,
You from the cedar-swamps, you from the pine,
You from the cotton and you from the vine,
You from the rice and the sugar-brakes,
You from the Rivers and you from the Lakes,
You from the Creeks and you from the Licks
And you from the brown bayou—
You and you and you—
You from the pulpit, you from the mine,
You from the factories, you from the banks,
Closer and closer, ranks on ranks,
Airplanes and cannon, and rifles and tanks,
Smith and Robinson, Brown and Jones,
Ruddy faces or bleaching bones,
After the turmoil and blood and pain
Swinging home to the folks again
Or sleeping alone in the fine French rain—
Every one of you won the war.

Every one of you won the war—
You and you and you—
Pressing and pouring forth, more and more,
Toiling and straining from shore to shore
To reach the flaming edge of the dark

Where man in his millions went up like a spark,
You, in your thousands and millions coming,
All the sea ploughed with you, all the air humming,
All the land loud with you,
All our hearts proud with you,
All our souls bowed with the awe of your coming!

Where's the Arch high enough,
Lads, to receive you,
Where's the eye dry enough,
Dears, to perceive you,
When at last and at last in your glory you come,
Tramping home?

Every one of you won the war,
You and you and you—
You that carry an unscathed head,
You that halt with a broken tread,
And oh, most of all, you Dead, you Dead!

Lift up the Gates for these that are last,
That are last in the great Procession.
Let the living pour in, take possession,
Flood back to the city, the ranch, the farm,
The church and the college and mill,
Back to the office, the store, the exchange,
Back to the wife with the babe on her arm,
Back to the mother that waits on the sill,
And the supper that's hot on the range.

And now, when the last of them all are by,
Be the Gates lifted up on high
To let those Others in,
Those Others, their brothers, that softly tread,
That come so thick, yet take no ground,
That are so many, yet make no sound,
Our Dead, our Dead, our Dead!

O silent and secretly-moving throng,
In your fifty thousand strong,
Coming at dusk when the wreaths have dropt,
And streets are empty, and music stopt,
Silently coming to hearts that wait
Dumb in the door and dumb at the gate,
And hear your step and fly to your call—
Every one of you won the war,
But you, you Dead, most of all!

[November 1918] (1919)

Even after the war, Wharton remained conscious of the sacrifices made in order to secure peace. It is particularly poignant, once peace has returned to a landscape healed from the war, to imagine the young soldiers forever deprived of their future. When she writes of the roses and myrtles, while Wharton is surely describing flowers of southern France, she would also be aware that both flowers were sacred to the goddess Aphrodite, goddess of love. The "young dead" died before they could experience the full flower of love.

🐛 Elegy

Ah, how I pity the young dead who gave
All that they were, and might become, that we
With tired eyes should watch this perfect sea
Re-weave its patterning of silver wave
Round scented cliffs of arbutus and bay.

No more shall any rose along the way,
The myrtled way that wanders to the shore,
Nor jonquil-twinkling meadow any more,
Nor the warm lavender that takes the spray,
Smell only of sea-salt and the sun,

But, through recurring seasons, every one
Shall speak to us with lips the darkness closes,
Shall look at us with eyes that missed the roses,
Clutch us with hands whose work was just begun,
Laid idle now beneath the earth we tread—

And always we shall walk with the young dead—
Ah, how I pity the young dead, whose eyes
Strain through the sod to see these perfect skies,
Who feel the new wheat springing in their stead,
And the lark singing for them overhead!

[?] (1920)

Toward the end of the war, in January 1919, Theodore Roosevelt died, at home, of natural causes. Wharton had known the president for many years, and she shared this elegy first with his family. Later it was published in the *Saturday Evening Post* and reprinted many times. The legend, from the Haida people, was recorded in Sir James Frazer's *The Golden Bough*; Wharton's personal copy of the book is marked at that spot. In stanza four she invokes: "Your last-born, and the dear loves of your heart": Roosevelt's youngest son, Quentin, was killed in the war. His first wife, Alice, and his mother, Martha, died on Valentine's Day 1884, within hours of each other. Alice was only twenty-two and his mother forty-eight at the time of their deaths. The imagery of ships suits Roosevelt well, who had been assistant secretary of the Navy.

🐚 With the Tide*

SOMEWHERE I read, in an old book whose name
Is gone from me, I read that when the days
Of a man are counted and his business done,
There comes up the shore at evening, with the tide,
To the place where he sits, a boat—
And in the boat, from the place where he sits, he sees
Dim in the dusk, dim and yet so familiar,
The faces of his friends long dead; and knows
They come for him, brought in upon the tide,
To take him where men go at set of day.

---

* I have chosen for the text the version of this poem that appears in *Twelve Poems* (1926), Wharton's final revision of it, which differs slightly in language and punctuation from its initial publication in the *Saturday Evening Post*.

Then, rising, with his hands in theirs, he goes
Between them his last steps, that are the first
Of the new life; and with the tide they pass,
Their shaken sail grown small upon the moon.

Often I thought of this, and pictured me
How many a man who lives with throngs about him,
Yet straining in the twilight for that boat
Shall scarce make out one figure in the stern,
And that so faint, its features shall perplex him
With doubtful memories—and his heart hang back.

But others, rising as they see the sail
Increase upon the sunset, hasten down,
Hands out and eyes elated; for they see,
Head over head, crowding from bow to stern,
Repeopling their long loneliness with smiles,
The faces of their friends—and such go out
Content upon the ebb-tide, with safe hearts.

But never
To worker summoned when his day was done
Did mounting tide bear such a freight of friends
As stole to you up the white wintry shingle
That night while those that watched you thought you slept.
Softly they came, and beached the boat, and stood
In the still cove, under the icy stars,
Your last-born and the dear loves of your heart,
And with them all the friends you called by name,
And all men that have loved right more than ease,

And honour above honours; all who gave
Free-handed of their best for other men,
And thought the giving taking; they who knew
Man's natural state is effort: up and up—
All these were there, so great a company
Perchance you marvelled, wondering what great craft
Had brought that throng unnumbered to the cove
Where the boys used to beach their light canoe
After old happy picnics.

But these your friends and children, to whose hands,
Committed in the silent night you rose
And took your last faint steps—
These led you down, O great American,
Down to the winter night and the white beach;
And there you saw that the huge hull that waited
Was not as are the boats of the other dead,
Frail craft for a light passage;
But first of a long line of towering ships,
Storm-worn and Ocean-weary every one,
The ships you launched, the ships you manned, the ships
That now, returning from their sacred quest
With the thrice-sacred burden of their dead,
Lay waiting there to take you forth with them,
Out on the flood-tide, to some farther quest.

[1919] (1919)

Nature's Lure

It would be hard to call Wharton a nature poet—she did not write pastoral poems about rural life, nor did she appear, at least until her old age, to have a spiritual bond with the natural world in the same way as the Romantic poets, whom she admired. Nevertheless, she observed her surroundings carefully and her imagination was captured from time to time by autumn scenes, sunsets, and afternoons in the countryside. From her earliest work we can find resonances drawn from nature and, in later years, a greater appreciation for simply inhabiting the outdoors.

Edith Jones

Who wrote these verses, she this volume owns,
Her unpoetic name is Edith Jones —

The inscription in Wharton's own copy of *Verses*,
privately published when she was sixteen and still Edith Jones.

Wharton's parents included this poem, written when Edith was fourteen, in *Verses*. The young poet was already adept at creating musical verse with unusual rhyme and stanza form and at encompassing complicated ideas about nature, the seasons, God, and art. If she owes something to Tennyson's "Flower in the crannied wall," we can honor her for being so well-read at such a young age.

Prophecies of Summer

I FOUND a wee leaf in the cleft
Where the half-melted ice had left
A sunny corner, moist and warm,
For it to bud, beyond all harm.
     The wet, brown sod,
Long horned with ice, had slowly grown
So soft, the tender seedling blown
By Autumn winds, in earliest Spring
Sent through the sun-warmed covering,
     Its little leaf to God.

I found it there, beneath a ledge,
The dawning Spring time's fairest pledge,
And to my mind it dimly brought
The sudden, joyous, leafy thought
     Of Summer-time.
I plucked it from the sheltered cleft
Which the more kindly ice had left.

Within my hand to drop and die,
But for its sweet suggestions, I
    Revive it in a rhyme.

[1876] (1878)

As we have seen in previous sections, Wharton often mourned the loss of what she saw as the grandeur and thrill of ancient times. Here she uses a flower, the violet, to reflect on that loss. In Greek mythology, violets were associated with Athens, which was sometimes referred to as "the violet-crowned city." Additionally Artemis, goddess of chastity and of the hunt, was said to have turned one of her maidens into a violet so that the girl could evade pursuit by Apollo. Hylas, a beautiful lad and a favorite of Heracles, decorated himself with floral wreaths, as did the dryads. Wharton weaves all of these legends of violets into her contemplation of one flower, even as she practices the unusual rhythm of dactylic meter.

🌺 Dactylics

VIOLET, lone of thy kind, on a delicate stem
Swaying thy pendulous crest in the breeze of the sea,
Thou to my backlooking eyes art a vagrant astray,
Wandering o'er acres of foam, by the blue of the wave
Borne from the uplands Egean and Attic ravines,
Where in the magical dawn of a happier day
Artemis trod thee, with footsteps agleam in the grass
White as twin daffodils beat by the low-walking wind
Hylas in garlands enwound thee to sweeten his hair
Laughing the Dryads in hollows of fern plume and furze
Move thee in links amethystine to wind through the dance
Or, in the Athens of Pericles, purple above,
Brows of the banqueters dripped thy mellifluous rain.

Now, on the Dryadless shore, in this laughterless air,
Lifting thy head uncompanioned thou seemest to say,

"Where are the uplands Egean, the Attic ravines,
Hylas, the Dryads?"

O Violet, here in my heart.

[1889–93] (2019)

Like "Dactylics," this poem appears in Wharton's poetry notebook, suggesting it was written during her early married years. Since it is titled for a mythical forest creature, one wonders whether the poem arises from her imagination or from close observation of a woodland scene.

Faun's Song

How golden-clear the sunlight shines
Through the long stretch of river-reeds.
The water whirls in splintering lines
As round the knotted thorn it speeds,
Then lapses to a tranquil pool,
Where water-spiders spin and sleep,
And yellow flower-de-luces cool
Their roots in shadowy moisture deep.

How still it is, how warm and still!
The wood is full of myriad noises
From tiny insect-throats that fill
The noonday heat with quivering voices—
How sweet it is to lie and dream,
Deep, deep, in stream-fed reeds and grass,
And see along the gliding stream
The gliding sunlight pause and pass!

[1890–93] (2019)

In this poem about perspective, notice how closely Wharton observes the woodland world she describes, from the tiny ants and beetles to the vast realm of the sun and the stars.

🐛 In the Forest

THE OAK.
Pale violet, perched upon my cushioned foot,
In the deep bracken's warm obscurity,
With head scarce raised above your trailing root,
    What is it that you see?

THE VIOLET.
I see, O lovely tree,
The earth's brown breast, o'ergrown
With all sweet blossoms blown;
The hastening ants for me
A friendly circuit make,
And sometimes, for their sake,
Beneath my leaves I hide
A little store of food;
All round, the joyous brood
Of wind-flowers open wide;
The odorous ferns upcurl
Each tenderly-furred frond;
A cricket's leap beyond,
Eve's primroses unfurl
Their pallour to the dusk;
A beetle keeps concealed

The forage of the field
In this brown chestnut-husk;
Haunt of the amorous bees
This towering foxglove springs,
And tells us humbler things
Of all she hears and sees;
Or in the long June days
Some starlit butterfly
Comes loitering idly by,
With gossiping delays;
(The little ones that dance
Like motes along the light,
In a foolish yellow flight,
Are never worth a glance)
And when the nights are warm,
And not a breath is shed
Through the green roof o'er head,
A velvet-pinioned swarm
Of moths (the bats of flowers)
Float through the brooding air,
And many a tale they bear
From other woods to ours.
But tell me lovely tree,
With your innumerous leafage branching wide,
Aloft above the kindly earth enskied,
      What is it that you see?

THE OAK.
I see the birth and ebbing of the stars
That in the populous heavens fall and rise;

Earliest for me the Summer day unbars
The dreaming twilight of the Eastern skies;
I see the veil of gradual rain close-drawn
Across the tranquil brightness of the sky.
The bloodless glare of many a stormy dawn,
The thunder-clouds at eve battalioned high;
And, as a flooring for the tempest's tread
When the wild winds are summoned from their sleep,
I see the lowlier forest round me spread
With branches surging like the troubled deep;
But I, far over all their boughs, have sight
Of star-communing peaks that shine alone;
First to receive and last to yield the light,
The moving clouds' immovable white throne;
And further still, on clearest days serene,
When sunlight on the peaks and woodland lies,
And a blue shadow holds the vale between,
I see, remote and melding with the skies,
The silver sea, whose shining distance knows
The thundering melody of ceaseless gales,
And borne upon whose tide my vision goes,
Beyond the searching of the swiftest sails.

[1889–93] (2019)

Scribner's Monthly published this poem in 1880, when Wharton, then Edith Jones, was eighteen. St. Martin's summer is the European equivalent of the American Indian summer. St. Martin's Day is November 11, and it traditionally ends the warm, lingering days. The poem is one sentence fit masterfully into the Petrarchan sonnet form, and it is one of her earliest mature pieces. It was reprinted numerous times in the years that followed, but until recently no one realized that Edith Jones was Edith Wharton.

St. Martin's Summer

AFTER the summer's fierce and thirsty glare,
  After the falling leaves and falling rain,
  When harsh winds beat the fields of ripened grain
And autumn's pennons from the branches flare,
There comes a stilly season, soft and fair,
  When clouds are lifted, winds are hushed again,—
  A phantom Summer hovering without pain
In the veiled radiance of the quiet air;
When, folding down the line of level seas,
  A silver mist at noonday faintly broods,
And like becalmèd ships the yellow trees
  Stand islanded in the windless solitudes,
Each leaf unstirred and parching for the breeze
  That hides and lingers northward in the woods.

[1880?] (1880)

From her poetry notebook of the early 1890s comes another fall poem. This could be called a modified rhyme royal, or seven-line stanza with ten syllables per line. Wharton enjoyed playing with sound and verse forms even as she created atmospheric poems. Biographers have suggested that Wharton did not enjoy living in Newport because the sea air made her feel ill, but this poem joins others arguing for her love of the sea.

🎵 October in Newport

GREY rocks, that lean against this perfect sky
And measureless expanse of silver sea;
Slow clouds of Autumn, poising calm and high
In windless depths of blue tranquility;
    Thwart cedar-boughs, that show
How long and bitterly the storm-winds blow
When Winter lays its hand upon the lea;

Brown hollows, tapestried with purple plume
Of late-blown asters, golden-rod's light head;
And the pale mallow's evanescent bloom,
No sooner loosened to the light than shed;
    Dark alders, close beset
With scarlet beads, and roses lingering yet
Though all your Summer sisterhood has fled,

And, O thou sea, winged with a fleet of dreams,
An argosy of longings, fairer far
Than any charmèd fishing-sail that gleams

At eventide against the sunset's bar,
	When the new moon holds sway
Above the darkling spaces of the day,
And the red West shakes forth a sudden star,

Lo, to these eyes that loved you from their birth,
No dreaming isle in waters hyaline,
No happy valley of this radiant earth,
No snow-wrapt peaks that tower above the pine,
	Lords of the lonely air,
Though for a crown the very dawn they wear,
With your transfiguring light shall ever shine.

[1889–93] (2005)

Another fall day, another warm sun, but a quite different feeling suffuses this autumn sonnet found in the same poetry notebook.

🐝 A November Day

WHEN earth has yielded to the wind and rain,
Drop after drop, the life-blood of her prime,
And, like a corpse beneath a shroud of rime,
Dark, cold and colourless her limbs have lain,
See how she draws bewildered breath again
On days like this, the interludes of Time,
When, waked anew to some diviner clime,
Faintly she smiles between the throes of pain.

Close as a lover stoops the watchful sky,
Like lover's arms the soothing sea enfolds
Earth's weariness—till it seems sweet to lie
So softly cradled in so warm a hold,
And the sick earth, forgetting she must die,
Would buy new beauties with the sun's last gold.

[1889–93] (2019)

Wharton composed this spring poem in 1892, in Italy. Note how she plays with repetition in the final line of each stanza.

Song

COME, for the leaf is alight on the bough,
Like a bird from the blue still aquiver from flight,
And but now was the day of the crocus, but now
With wind-flowers the mould of the woodland was white;
April's here, Spring is here, hope is on the wing!

Come, for the primroses spangle the slope
By the stream that is red from the rush of the rains,
And the footstep in drifts of dead oak-leaves agrope
May bruise the anemone's exquisite veins;
April's here, hope is here, now's the heart of Spring!

Part the dead pine-needles—lo, the live grass!
Mark, where the clouds break, the burst of the blue—
Through the old brambles young ivy-shoots pass,
And after each shower the world's born anew.
April's here, Spring is here, hope is on the wing!
April's here, hope is here, now's the heart of Spring!

[1892] (2019)

The next two complementary poems appear back-to-back early in Wharton's poetry notebook. The epigraph to "The Southwind" comes from the Bible, the Song of Solomon (4:16), where it is used as an invitation to the beloved to enter a garden. Wharton chooses different meters to suit the feel of the different winds.

The Northwind

FORTH from the north with a thunder of wings
Leap, O thou longed-for, to gladden our eyes,
Scatter the sea-mist that lingers and clings,
Sweep the last cloud from the scintillant skies!
Long, long have we sought for the life thou has brought,
Thou Angel of healing, awake and arise!

Blithe as a bridegroom who springs to his bride,
Swift as a tiger who seizes his prey,
Dash the grey veil of the Southwind aside,
Bare the earth's breast to the eye of the day,
Yea, loosen the sleep of the mesmerized deep
And "let there be light!" to this shadowland say.

Freighted with balm of the balsam and pine,
Shot with the boreal blaze of the north,
Cold as the ice-bergs and heady as wine,
Bound from the lair of thy solitude forth,
From the trees in thy hold shake a ransom of gold,
Then scatter thy largesse of leaves o'er the earth.

Bid the bright hearth-fires leap in thy praise,
Laugh as we lean to the warmth of the flame,
Shout round the eaves of the sunless dark days
Northward, where daylight and night are the same,
Then sing with a cry of the midsummer sky
Where the sun, never setting, puts darkness to shame!

Bear us away in the wings of thy might
Far o'er the islands of granite and pine,
Till we behold, with the innermost sight,
Ice-cliffs and chasms that darkle and shine,
Yea, fill up our souls like wassailer's bowls,
With the fiery froth of thy rapturous wine!

[1889–93] (2019)

"Awake, O Northwind; and come, thou South."

❧ The Southwind

O SOUTHWIND, sliding over trancèd seas,
Gleaning from those grey meadows veiled in haze
Flowers of foam-born mist, with stealthy hand
  To wreathe the waiting land,
Garlands to weave between the languid trees
Like Lombard vines in old Virgilian days,

Southwind, thou alien on this arid shore,
Impearling with soft-scattered gems of dew
Smooth lawns and bearded pastures, where the feet
        Sink deep in meadowsweet,
And the lush bramble hedges spangled o'er
With wan wild-roses faint of scent and hue,

Thou that in other regions hast thy birth,
With flagging flight across the northern foam
By sunless islands girt with sullen rocks
        Against the Atlantic's shocks,
By leagues of bleak, inhospitable earth,
Whence have thy silver-sandalled footsteps come?

Glassing its palm-trees in the purple deep,
What island, fringed in foliage coralline,
Cradled thine infant breathings, ere the storm
        Summoned thee, moist and warm,
From the soft bosom of the South to leap
And, wandering northward, woo the stubborn pine?

What argosies before thine urging sped,
Laden with spices from a perfumed land,
And burnished oranges, the Golden Fleece
        Of these pale days of peace?
As Thetis once the sails of Jason led,
What homeward-reaching sails didst thou expand?

Magician of the Leucothean veil,
Transforming with thy mild assuaging breath

Our crystal skies and blithe victorious sea,
        Until we seem to be
Prisoned forever in the ghostly pale
Where speechless shadows walk the ways of death,

Thy murmur has the sound of far-off seas,
Sweeter than jasmine is thy dreamy mouth,
And he who yields him to thy faint embrace
        Sees, in his homestead's place,
Some halcyon island plumed with tropic trees
Asleep beneath the kisses of the South.

[1889–93] (2019)

Wharton first visited the medieval, turreted, and moated Bodiam Castle in 1908 with Henry James, and she recorded the moment in *A Backward Glance* many years later.

> One perfect afternoon we spent at Bodiam—my first visit there. It was still the old spell-bound ruin, unrestored, guarded by great trees, and by a network of lanes which baffled the invading charabancs [tour buses]. Tranquil white clouds hung above it in a windless sky, and the silence and solitude were complete as we sat looking across at the crumbling towers, and at their reflection in a moat starred with water-lilies, and danced over by great blue dragon-flies. For a long time no one spoke; then James turned to me and said solemnly: "Summer afternoon—summer afternoon; to me those have always been the two most beautiful words in the English language." They were the essence of that hushed scene, those ancient walls; and I never hear them spoken without seeing the towers of Bodiam mirrored in their enchanted moat. (249)

But does this poem, published in 1911, arise from that early visit, or from a subsequent one with her lover, Morton Fullerton?

🐦 Summer Afternoon (Bodiam Castle, Sussex)

NOT all the wasteful beauty of the year
Heaped in the scale of one consummate hour
Shall this outweigh: the curve of quiet air
That held, as in the green sun-fluted light
Of sea-caves quivering in a tidal lull,
Those trancèd towers and long unruined walls,
Moat-girdled from the world's dissolving touch,

The rook-flights lessening over evening woods,
And, down the unfrequented grassy slopes,
The shadows of old oaks contemplative
Reaching behind them like the thoughts of age.

High overhead hung the long Sussex ridge,
Sun-cinctured, as a beaker's rim of gold
Curves round its green concavity; and slow
Across the upper pastures of the sky
The clouds moved white before the herding airs
That in the hollow, by the moated walls,
Stirred not one sleeping lily from its sleep.

Deeper the hush fell; more remote the earth
Fled onward with the flight of cloud and sun,
And cities strung upon the flashing reel
Of nights and days. We knew no more of these
Than the grey towers redoubling in the moat
The image of a bygone strength transformed
To beauty's endless uses; and like them
We felt the touch of that renewing power
That turns the landmarks of man's ruined toil
To high star-haunted reservoirs of peace.
And with that sense there came the deeper sense
Of moments that, between the beats of time,
May thus insphere in some transcendent air
The plenitude of being.
Far currents feed them, from those slopes of soul
That know the rise and set of other stars
White-roaring downward through remote defiles

Dim-forested with unexplorèd thought;
Yet tawny from the flow of lower streams
That drink the blood of battle, sweat of earth,
And the broached vats of cities revelling.
All these the moments hold; yet these resolved
To such clear wine of beauty as shall flush
The blood to richer living. . . . Thus we mused,
And musing thus we felt the magic touch,
And such a moment held us. As, at times,
Through the long windings of each other's eyes
We have reached some secret hallowed silent place
That a god visits at the turn of night—
In such a solitude the moment held us.
And one were thought and sense in that profound
Submersion of all being deep below
The vexèd waves of action. Clear we saw,
Through the clear nether stillness of the place,
The gliding images of words and looks
Swept from us down the gusty tides of time,
And here unfolding to completer life;
And like dull pebbles from a sunless shore
Plunged into crystal waters, suddenly
We took the hues of beauty, and became,
Each to the other, all that each had sought.

Thus did we feel the moment and the place
One in the heart of beauty; while far off
The rooks' last cry died on the fading air,
And the first star stood white upon the hill.

[1908–11?] (1911)

The next two poems were written after the war. Wharton was in her sixties and had acquired a gracious home on the Riviera, where she had always loved to spend the winter. Her verse form is looser; her diction, while elevated, more contemporary; and her appreciation of the flowers and birds is more extravagant. A long, slow immersion into the natural world yields less imagining of the past and more present beauty and happiness. Once again, Wharton's love of the sounds of words is revealed by reading the poems aloud.

🎵 Nightingales in Provence

I

WHENCE come they, small and brown,
Miraculous and frail,
Like spring's invisible pollen blown
On the wild southern gale?
From whatsoever depth of gold and blue,
Far-templed sand and ringèd palms they wing,
Falling like dew
Upon the land, they bring
Music and spring,
With all things homely-sweet
Exhaled beneath the feet
On stony mountain-trail,
Or where green slopes, through tamarisk and pine,
Seaward decline—
Thyme and the lavender,
Where honey-bees make stir,

And the green dragon-flies with silver whirr
Loot the last rosemaries—
The morning-glory, rosy as her name,
The poppies' leaping flame
Along the kindled vines,
Down barren banks the vetches spilt like lees,
In watery meadows the great celandines
Afloat like elfin moons,
In the pale world of dunes
A foam of asphodel
Upon the sea's blue swell,
And, where the great rocks valley-ward are rolled,
The tasselled ilex-bloom fringing dark woods with gold.

Shyly the first begin—
And the thrilled ear delays,
Through a fresh veil of interblossomed mays
Straining to win
That soft sequestered note,
Where the new throat,
In some deep cleft of quietness remote,
Its budding bliss essays.
Shyly the first begin—
But, as the numerous rose
First to the hedgerow throws
A blossom here and there,
As if in hope to win
The unheeding glances of the passer-by,
And, never catching his dulled eye,
Thinks: "But my tryst is with the Spring!"

And suddenly the dusty roadside glows
With scented glory, crimsoned to its close—
So wing by wing,
Unheeded and unheard,
Bird after bird,
They come;
And where the woods were dumb,
Dumb all the streamsides and unlistening vales,
Now glory streams along the evening gales,
And all the midday is a murmuring,
Now they are come.

II

I lie among the thyme;
The sea is at my feet,
And all the air is sweet
With the capricious chime
Of interwoven notes
From those invisible and varying throats,
As though the blossomed trees,
The laden breeze,
The springs within their caves,
And even the sleeping waves,
Had all begun to sing.

Sweet, sweet, oh heavy-sweet
As tropic bales undone
At a Queen's ebon feet
In equatorial sun,

Those myriad balmy voices
Drip iterated song,
And every tiny tawny throat rejoices
To mix its separate rapture with the throng.
For now the world is theirs,
And the captivated airs
Carry no other note.
As from midsummer's throat,
Strong-pillared, organ-built,
Pours their torrential glory.
On their own waves they float,
And toss from crest to crest their cockle-shell of story—
And, as plumed breakers tilt
Against the plangent beaches,
And all the long reticulated reaches
Hiss with their silver lances,
And heave with their deep rustle of retreat
At fall of day—
So swells, and so withdraws that tidal lay
As spring advances. . . .

III

I lie among the thyme,
The sea is at my feet,
And the slow-kindling moon begins to climb
To her bejewelled seat—
And now, and now again,
Mixed with her silver rain,
Listen, a rarer strain,

A tenderer fall—
And all the night is white and musical,
The forests hold their breath, the sky lies still
On every listening hill,
And far far out those straining sails,
Even as they dip and turn,
One moment backward yearn
To the rich laughter of the nightingales.

[1919–26?] (1926)

The mistral is a strong, cold wind that blows through southern France in the winter; the maquis is the dense, scrub evergreen vegetation common to its coastal regions. The atmosphere of a coming storm is here evoked in religious terms.

🦋 Mistral in the Maquis

ROOFED in with creaking pines we lie
And see the waters burn and whiten,
The wild seas race the racing sky,
The tossing landscape gloom and lighten.

With emerald streak and silver blotch
The white wind paints the purple sea.
Warm in our hollow dune we watch
The honey-orchis nurse the bee.

Gold to the keel the startled boats
Beat in on palpitating sail,
While overhead with many throats
The choral forest hymns the gale.

'Neath forest-boughs the templed air
Hangs hushed as when the Host is lifted,
While, flanks astrain and rigging bare,
The last boat to the port has drifted. . . .

Nought left but the lost wind that grieves
On darkening seas and furling sails,

And the long light that Beauty leaves
Upon her fallen veils. . . .

[1919–26?] (1926)

Courtship, Love, and Heartbreak

Most poets write love poetry. Indeed Wharton, in her preface to the anthology *Eternal Passion in English Poetry*, observed that—with the notable exception of Shakespeare—"the rank taken by love-poems in the total production of each poet is almost always in inverse ratio to the greatness of the poet." While great poets can distill emotion and imagery from many sources, Wharton suggests, "minor poets reach their highest height in the love-poem" (vi).

Was this true for Wharton herself? Surely her poetry gained force and emotional depth during and after her love affair with the fickle, elusive Morton Fullerton. Earlier poems, written when she was in her teens and into her thirties, have a different feel about them, some more sentimental, others more satiric. The poems gathered here offer an ample representation, but by no means a complete record, of her love poetry from early days until old age.

These first three poems were written when Wharton was in her teens and gathered by her parents in *Verses*. We can see her interest in the subject of love, courtship, and loss, and we can also admire how astute was her understanding of life's possibilities and limitations, particularly for women. It is worth noting her sophisticated ability to create a persona, a speaker in the poem who is not the poet herself.

🎵 Some Woman to Some Man

WE might have loved each other after all,
Have lived and learned together! Yet I doubt it;
You asked, I think, too great a sacrifice,
Or else, perhaps, I rate myself too dear.
Whichever way the difference lies between us,
Would common cares have helped to lessen it,
A common interest, and a common lot?
Who knows indeed? We choose our path, and then
Stand looking back and sighing at our choice,
And say: "Perhaps the other road had led
To fruitful valleys dozing in the sun."
Perhaps—perhaps—but all things are perhaps,
And either way there lies a doubt, you know.
We've but one life to live, and fifty ways
To live it in, and little time to choose
The one in fifty that will suit us best,
And so the end is, that we part, and say:
"We might have loved each other after all!"

[1878] (1878)

🎵 A Woman I Know

FOR a look from her eyes, for a smile of her mouth
Any man might well give the best years of his youth;
For the touch of her hand, for the warmth of her kiss
Might well barter his chances of infinite bliss;

For her step is like sunlight that plays on the sea
And her bosom is snowy as snowy can be,
And her hair is a mantle inwoven with gold
Such as Queens might have worn in the legends of old;

And her chin oh so white, and her cheek oh so red,
They might well drive a man who should look at them mad;
But beneath the bright breast where her heart ought to be,
What is there? Why a trap to catch fools, sir, like me!

[October 1878] (1878)

Nothing More

'T was the old, old story told again,
   The story we all have heard;
A glimpse of brightness, parting and pain—
   You know it word for word.

A stolen picture—a faded rose—
   An evening hushed and bright;
A whisper—perhaps a kiss—who knows?
   A handclasp, and "goodnight."

The sum of what we call "first love,"
   That dreamflower rare and white,
That puts its magic blossom forth
   And dies in a single night.

[1878] (1878)

Bettina von Arnim (1785–1859) was a writer and noted figure of the German Romantic movement. As a child she was befriended by Goethe, by then a celebrated author in his fifties, and they began a correspondence that was later published. Wharton's brother Harry gave Edith a copy of the correspondence for Christmas when she was ten years old; the epigraph below comes from von Arnim's book. Wharton and her governess, Anna Bahlmann, loved Goethe and read his work together in the original German. At fourteen, Edith imagines the worshipful, chaste love a girl her age might have for a great poet.

🎵 Bettine to Goethe

"Be friendly, pray, with these fancies of mine."
—BETTINE

COULD youth discrown thy head of its gray hair,
I could not love it as I love it now;
Could one grand line be smoothed from thy brow,
'Twould seem to me less stately and less fair.
O no, be as thou art! For thou dost wear
The signs of noble age that cannot bow
Thine intellect like thy form, and I who know
How each year that did visibly impair
Thy first fresh youth, left inwardly such grand
And gracious gifts, would rather have thee so—
Believe me, master, who erect doth stand
In soul and purpose, age cannot lay low
Till he receive, new from the Father's hand
The youth he did but outwardly forego.

[April 1876] (1878)

As a young girl, Wharton, as Edith Jones, continued to write poetry, the one form of literature open to young ladies in her day. When she was eighteen, her brother sent a handful of her poems to a friend of his who had just purchased the *North American Review*. The friend sent them on to the good gray poet Henry Wadsworth Longfellow (1807–1882), who in turn offered them to William Dean Howells (1837–1920), editor of *The Atlantic Monthly*. Howells published them over several months. On the theme of love lost, both of these poems reveal an awareness of the passivity of a woman and the necessity of hiding her true feelings.

A Failure

(*She speaks.*)

I MEANT to be so strong and true!
    The world may smile and question, When?
But what I might have been to you
    I cannot be to other men.
Just one in twenty to the rest,
    And all in all to you alone,—
This was my dream; perchance 't is best
    That this, like other dreams, is flown.

For you I should have been so kind,
    So prompt my spirit to control,
To win fresh vigor for my mind,
    And purer beauties for my soul;
Beneath your eye I might have grown
    To that divine, ideal height,

Which, mating wholly with your own,
    Our equal spirits should unite.

To others I am less than naught;
    To you I might have been so much,
Could but your calm, discerning thought
    Have put my powers to the touch!
Your love had made me doubly fair;
    Your wisdom made me thrice as wise,
Lent clearer lustre to my hair,
    And read new meanings in my eyes.

Ah, yes, to you I might have been
    That happy being, past recall,
The slave, the helpmeet, and the queen,—
    All these in one, and one in all.
But that which I had dreamed to do
    I learned too late was dreamed in vain,
For what I might have been to you
    I cannot be to other men.

[1879–80] (1880)

🐝 The Parting Day

I

SOME busy hands have brought to light,
    And laid beneath my eye,
The dress I wore that afternoon
    You came to say good-by.

About it still there seems to cling
    Some fragrance unexpressed,
The ghostly odor of the rose
    I wore upon my breast;

And, subtler than all flower-scent,
    The sacred garment holds
The memory of that parting day
    Close hidden in its folds.

The rose is dead, and you are gone,
    But to the dress I wore
The rose's smell, the thought of you,
    Are wed forevermore.

II

That day you came to say good-by
    (A month ago! It seems a year!)

How calm I was! I met your eye,
    And in my own you saw no tear.

You heard me laugh and talk and jest,
    And lightly grieve that you should go;
You saw the rose upon my breast,
    But not the breaking heart below.

And when you came and took my hand,
    It scarcely fluttered in your hold.
Alas, you did not understand!
    For you were blind, and I was cold.

And now you cannot see my tears,
    And now you cannot hear my cry.
A month ago? Nay, years and years
    Have aged my heart since that good-by.

[1879–80] (1880)

This unpublished poem, probably written when Wharton was in her thirties, speaks of lifelong love, with a kind of nostalgia for the future. Its musicality is exceptional; its verse form is close to a Spanish *sextilla*, which calls for six-line stanzas of eight syllables each, rhymed *abbaba*. When we read the poem aloud, the cadences and the repetition of sound deepen the mood of the poem and the tension of love versus the inexorability of age and death.

🐚 Song

LET us be lovers to the end,
O you to whom my soul is given,
Whose smiles have turned this earth to heaven,
Fast holding hands as we descend
Life's pathway devious and uneven,
Let us be lovers to the end.

Dear, let us make of Time a friend
To bind us closer with his cares,
And though grief strike us unawares
No poisoned shaft that fate can send
Shall wound us through each other's prayers,
If we are lovers to the end.

Let us be lovers to the end
And, growing blind as we grow old,
Refuse forever to behold
How age has made the shoulders bend

And Winter blanched the hair's young gold.
Let us be lovers to the end.

Whichever way our footsteps tend
Be sure that, if we walk together,
They'll lead to realms of sunny weather,
By shores where quiet waters wend.
At eventide we shall go thither,
If we are lovers to the end.

[1889–93] (2019)

A little poem most likely written when Wharton was in her late twenties or early thirties.

A LITTLE while, My Sweet,
Love holds our linkèd feet
In rosy chains together;
Then comes the Wintry weather—
The roses fall and fade,
And lo our feet have strayed,
Have strayed we know not whither—

[1889–93] (2019)

Wharton read and admired sonnets more than any other verse form. This gem, written when she was in her twenties, uses words to argue against the adequacy of words and for the power of silence. Note how she has learned to use the "turn" between octave and sestet. The last line echoes Psalm 42.

❧ Happiness

THIS perfect love can find no words to say.
What words are left, still sacred for our use,
That have not suffered the sad world's abuse,
And figure forth a gladness dimmed and gray?
Let us be silent still, since words convey
But shadowed images, wherein we lose
The fulness of love's light; our lips refuse
The fluent commonplace of yesterday.

Then shall we hear beneath the brooding wing
Of silence what abiding voices sleep,
The primal notes of nature, that outring
Man's little noises, warble he or weep,
The song the morning stars together sing,
The sound of deep that calleth unto deep.

[?] (1889)

This poem of lost love appears early in Wharton's poetry notebook. Perhaps it was another exercise in musicality: its dactylic meter is more often used for light verse. In any case, while charming, the poem does not have the weight of those written after her own heart had experienced cruelty, betrayal, and loss.

🪶 Song

MIRTH of life's blooming time, sweet beyond seeming,
Lilies that laugh with the dews of the morning,
Grasses that glitter with gifts of the rain,
Roses like kisses, and kisses as fragrant
As roses that cradle June's velvet-barred vagrant,
All these I had of thee when I was glad of thee,
Now thou art gone from me, what shall remain?

Blush of the sunrise and blaze of the sunset,
Stars that are born of the gloom after moonset,
Planets that swim in the sea of the dusk,
Bird-song like laughter, and laughter as thrilling
As all the dawn's rapture of jubilant trilling,
All these I had of thee when I was glad of thee,
Now the fruit's eaten, I hold but the husk.

[1889–93] (2005)

Wharton's love poetry changed dramatically during and after her romance with the American journalist Morton Fullerton. Many of the following poems refer specifically to days and nights she spent with him. Wharton was, of course, married, and Fullerton was simultaneously carrying on affairs with numerous women (and a few men), so their affair could never fulfill her dreams of what love ought to be. Although we must assume that as a writer Wharton was able to distance herself from the "I" of the poem, it would be impossible to read these poems without some awareness of the autobiographical impulse. She was above all an artist, but we must ask who was the audience for these poems? Some she sent to Fullerton, most she wrote in her private journal and chose not to publish. All of the following poems are infused with the intensity of her complicated feelings about this man who changed her inner life forever, and her feelings about herself as well. Often the heartbreak is already embedded in the expressions of love.

The next three poems come from the private diary Wharton started when her love for Fullerton began to blossom. "Ame Close" means the private, or closed, soul, and is the name she used for her private diary about Fullerton.

Ame Close

MY SOUL is like a house that dwellers nigh
Can see no light in. "Ah, poor house," they say,
"Long since its owners died or went their way.
Thick ivy loops the rusted door-latch tie,
The chimney rises cold against the sky,
And flowers turned weed down the bare path's decay . . ."

Yet one stray passer, at the shut of day,
Sees a light tremble in a casement high.

Even so, my soul would set a light for you,
A light invisible to all beside,
As though a lover's ghost should yearn and glide
From pane to pane, to let the flame shine through.
Yet enter not, lest, as it flits ahead,
You see the hand that carries it is dead.

[February 21, 1908] (1994)

This poem commemorates Wharton and Fullerton's 1908 outing to Senlis, a town north of Paris. Two versions of the poem exist, one in a manuscript in Fullerton's hand and the other in Wharton's love diary. Verse three is written, then crossed out, in the diary, indicating that Wharton could still step back and edit her work, remaining an artist even in love.

🎵 Senlis. May 16th

HUNG high against the perfect blue,
Like flame the belfry trembled higher,
Like leafage let the bird-flights through,
Like incense wreathed its melting spire.

From the dim vantage, lilac-hung,
Niched in the Roman rampart's strength,
We watched the foaming clouds that swung
Against the church's island-length;

[The sheet of emerald foliage spread
Like some deep inlet's inmost reach,
Between the cliff-like towers o'erhead,
The low slate roofs that formed their beach.]

We watched, and felt the tides of time
Coil round our hidden leafy place,
Sweep on through changing race and clime,
And leave us at the heart of space,

In some divine transcendent hush
Where light and darkness melt and cease,
Staying the awful cosmic rush
To give two hearts an hour of peace. . . .

So deep the peace, so ours the hour,
When night-fall and the fiery train
Had swept us from our high-built bower,
And out across the dreaming plain,

Stillness yet brooded in our souls,
And even our rushing chariot stayed,
Loitering through aisles of silvery boles,
In some remote and star-laced glade,

Where, through the pale and secret night,
Past gleams of water, depths of shade,
Under a low moon's golden light
We felt the quiet fields outspread—

And there, on the calm air afloat,
While silence held the throbbing train,
Some thrush from immemorial throat
Poured all the sweetness, all the pain.—

[May 17, 1908] (1994)

Later that month Wharton parted temporarily from Fullerton, who remained in France as she sailed home to America to meet her husband. She wrote this poem while at sea and included it in her love diary.

WHEN I am gone, recall my hair,
Not for the light it used to hold,
But that your touch, enmeshèd there,
Has turned it to a younger gold.

Recall my hands, that were not soft
Or white or fine beyond expressing,
Till they had slept so long and oft,
So warm and close, in your possessing.

Recall my eyes, that used to lie
Blind pools with summer's wreckage strewn.
You cleared the drift, but in their sky
You hung no image but your own.

Recall my mouth, that knew not how
A kiss is cradled and takes wing,
Yet fluttered like a nest-hung bough
When you had touched it like the Spring. . . .

[May 25, 1908] (1975)

This poem exists in Fullerton's transcription of it, with his explanatory note following. After Fullerton's death, the document was presented by his cousin to the Wharton scholars Marion Mainwaring and R. W. B. Lewis, who authenticated it and purchased it for the Yale University Library archives. The poem's move from the beauty of lovemaking to the ashes of separation shocks the reader.

Terminus

WONDERFUL was the long secret night you gave me, my
　　Lover,
Palm to palm, breast to breast in the gloom. The faint red lamp,
Flushing with magical shadows the common-place room of the
　　inn,
With its dull impersonal furniture, kindled a mystic flame
In the heart of the swinging mirror, the glass that has seen
Faces innumerous and vague of the endless travelling automata,
Whirled down the ways of the world like dust-eddies swept
　　through a street
Faces indifferent or weary, frowns of impatience or pain,
Smiles (if such there were ever) like your smile and mine when
　　they met
Here, in this self-same glass, while you helped me to loosen my
　　dress,
And the shadow-mouths melted to one, like sea-birds that meet
　　in a wave—
Such smiles, yes, such smiles the mirror perhaps has reflected;
And the low wide bed, as rutted and worn as a high-road,
The bed with its soot-sodden chintz, the grime of its brasses

That has borne the weight of fagged bodies, dust-stained,
      averted in sleep.
The hurried, the restless, the aimless—perchance it has also
      thrilled
With the pressure of bodies ecstatic, bodies like ours,
Seeking each other's souls in the depths of unfathomed caresses,
And through the long windings of passion emerging again to the
      stars. . . .
Yes, all this through the room, the passive and featureless room,
Must have flowed with the rise and fall of the human unceasing
      current;
And lying there hushed in your arms, as the waves of rapture
      receded,
And far down the margin of being we heard the low beat of the
      soul,
I was glad as I thought of those others, the nameless, the many,
Who perhaps thus had lain and loved for an hour on the brink
      of the world,
Secret and fast in the heart of the whirlwind of travel,
The shaking and shrieking of trains, the night-long shudder of
      traffic,
Thus, like us they have lain and felt, breast to breast in the dark
The fiery rain of possession descend on their limbs while out-
      side
The black rain of midnight pelted the roof of the station;
And thus some woman like me, waking alone before dawn,
While her lover slept, as I woke and heard the calm stir of your
      breathing

Some woman has heard as I heard the farewell shriek of the
       trains
Crying good-bye to the city and staggering out into darkness,
And shaken at heart has thought: "So must we forth in the
       darkness,
Sped down the fixed rail of habit by the hand of implacable
       fate—
So shall we issue to life, and the rain, and the dull dark dawning;
You to the wide flare of cities, with windy garlands and shout-
       ing,
Carrying to populous places the freight of holiday throngs;
I, by waste lands, and stretches of low-skied marsh
To a harbourless wind-bitten shore, where a dull town moulders
       and shrinks,
And its roofs fall in, and the sluggish feet of the hours
Are printed in grass in its streets; and between the featureless
       houses
Languid the town-folk glide to stare at the entering train,
The train from which no one descends; till one pale evening of
       winter,
When it halts on the edge of the town, see, the houses have
       turned into grave-stones,
The streets are the grassy-paths between the low roofs of the
       dead;
And as the train glides in ghosts stand by the doors of the car-
       riages;
And scarcely the difference is felt—Yea, such is the life I return
       to . . ."

Thus may another have thought; thus, as I turned may have
     turned
To the sleeping lips at her side, to drink, as I drank there,
     oblivion. . . .

[Poem written by E.W. during my month in America, and commemo-
rating, in the inspiration of Goethe's Roman Elegies, the night which
we spent at Charing Cross Hotel, before I sailed from Southampton.
We had motored from Paris to Boulogne, and crossed to Folkestone
when we passed the night. On the morrow we went up to London,
and were met at dinner by Henry James. I took an appartment [*sic*]
^two chambers and salon^ no 92, in which I left her alone the next
day at 10:00 with only time to have sent to her room a bunch of roses.
That evening at sea I received the accompanying telegram. M.F. 1909]

[1909] (1975)

As with many of Wharton's love poems written during the time of her Fullerton affair, these next two sonnets enmesh earthly love with ideal love and embed heartbreak within passion. This one also came from Fullerton, who noted on the bottom: "E.W. after her visit chez moi 15 April 1910."

SHE said to me: "Nay, take my body and eat,
And give it beauty, breaking it for bread.
Or else, your hunger sated, drain instead
The chalice of my soul, wherein, to meet
Your longed-for lips, the bitter and the sweet
Of passion's mystic vintage have been shed,
And through the clear cold crystals of the head
Tremble the ardours of the central heat."

She said: "Your thirst appeasèd, rest you yet
A quiet moment in the thought of me . . .
Then pass upon your way, and quite forget;
Or dimly—as one inland feels the sea—
Recall that once a summer hour long set
Hung over you the murmur of leaf and bee . . .

[April 15, 1910] (2004)

In the middle of her affair with Fullerton, ever the savvy writer, Wharton sought to publish a volume of poetry, telling her editor she had begun again to "warble." *Artemis to Actæon* appeared in April 1909, and in it she included three love poems, presented here in the order in which she placed them in that volume. They are more formal in their language and elevated in thought, and their audience is clearly a public one rather than solely herself or the beloved.

Wharton and Fullerton often recited poetry together. The title of the following sonnet sequence, written for Fullerton, alludes to George Meredith's ironic sonnet sequence "Modern Love" (poem XXIX):

> "I cannot be at peace
> In having Love upon a mortal lease."

🐚 The Mortal Lease

I

BECAUSE the currents of our love are poured
Through the slow welter of the primal flood
From some blind source of monster-haunted mud,
And flung together by random forces stored
Ere the vast void with rushing worlds was scored—
Because we know ourselves but the dim scud
Tossed from their heedless keels, the sea-blown bud
That wastes and scatters ere the wave has roared—

Because we have this knowledge in our veins,
Shall we deny the journey's gathered lore—

The great refusals and the long disdains,
The stubborn questing for a phantom shore,
The sleepless hopes and memorable pains,
And all mortality's immortal gains?

II

Because our kiss is as the moon to draw
The mounting waters of that red-lit sea
That circles brain with sense, and bids us be
The playthings of an elemental law,
Shall we forego the deeper touch of awe
On love's extremest pinnacle, where we,
Winging the vistas of infinity,
Gigantic on the mist our shadows saw?

Shall kinship with the dim first-moving clod
Not draw the folded pinion from the soul,
And shall we not, by spirals vision-trod,
Reach upward to some still-retreating goal,
As earth, escaping from the night's control,
Drinks at the founts of morning like a god?

III

All, all is sweet in that commingled draught
Mysterious, that life pours for lovers' thirst,
And I would meet your passion as the first
Wild woodland woman met her captor's craft,
Or as the Greek whose fearless beauty laughed

And doffed her raiment by the Attic flood;
But in the streams of my belated blood
Flow all the warring potions love has quaffed.

How can I be to you the nymph who danced
Smooth by Ilissus as the plane-tree's bole,
Or how the Nereid whose drenched lashes glanced
Like sea-flowers through the summer sea's long roll—
I that have also been the nun entranced
Who night-long held her Bridegroom in her soul?

IV

"Sad Immortality is dead," you say,
"And all her grey brood banished from the soul;
Life, like the earth, is now a rounded whole,
The orb of man's dominion. Live to-day."
And every sense in me leapt to obey,
Seeing the routed phantoms backward roll;
But from their waning throng a whisper stole,
And touched the morning splendour with decay.

"Sad Immortality is dead; and we
The funeral train that bear her to her grave.
Yet hath she left a two-faced progeny
In hearts of men, and some will always see
The skull beneath the wreath, yet always crave
In every kiss the folded kiss to be."

V

Yet for one rounded moment I will be
No more to you than what my lips may give,
And in the circle of your kisses live
As in some island of a storm-blown sea,
Where the cold surges of infinity
Upon the outward reefs unheeded grieve,
And the loud murmur of our blood shall weave
Primeval silences round you and me.

If in that moment we are all we are
We live enough. Let this for all requite.
Do I not know, some wingèd things from far
Are borne along illimitable night
To dance their lives out in a single flight
Between the moonrise and the setting star?

VI

The Moment came, with sacramental cup
Lifted—and all the vault of life grew bright
With tides of incommensurable light—
But tremblingly I turned and covered up
My face before the wonder. Down the slope
I heard her feet in irretrievable flight,
And when I looked again, my stricken sight
Saw night and rain in a dead world agrope.

Now walks her ghost beside me, whispering
With lips derisive: "Thou that wouldst forego—
What god assured thee that the cup I bring
Globes not in every drop the cosmic show,
All that the insatiate heart of man can wring
From life's long vintage?—Now thou shalt not know."

VII

Shall I not know? I, that could always catch
The sunrise in one beam along the wall,
The nests of June in April's mating call,
And ruinous autumn in the wind's first snatch
At summer's green impenetrable thatch—
That always knew far off the secret fall
Of a god's feet across the city's brawl,
The touch of silent fingers on my latch?

Not thou, vain Moment! Something more than thou
Shall write the score of what mine eyes have wept,
The touch of kisses that have missed my brow,
The murmur of wings that brushed me while I slept,
And some mute angel in the breast even now
Measures my loss by all that I have kept.

VIII

Strive we no more. Some hearts are like the bright
Tree-chequered spaces, flecked with sun and shade,
Where gathered in old days the youth and maid

To woo, and weave their dances; with the night
They cease their flutings, and the next day's light
Finds the smooth green unconscious of their tread,
And ready its velvet pliancies to spread
Under fresh feet, till these in turn take flight.

But other hearts a long long road doth span,
From some far region of old works and wars,
And the weary armies of the thoughts of man
Have trampled it, and furrowed it with scars,
And sometimes, husht, a sacred caravan
Moves over it alone, beneath the stars.

[1909] (1909)

⚘ Survival

WHEN you and I, like all things kind or cruel,
The garnered days and light evasive hours,
Are gone again to be a part of flowers
And tears and tides, in life's divine renewal,

If some grey eve to certain eyes should wear
A deeper radiance than mere light can give,
Some silent page abruptly flush and live,
May it not be that you and I are there?

[December 14, 1908] (1909)

🐛 A Meeting

On a sheer peak of joy we meet;
    Below us hums the abyss;
Death either way allures our feet
    If we take one step amiss.

One moment let us drink the blue
    Transcendent air together—
Then down where the same old work's to do
    In the same dull daily weather.

We may not wait . . . yet look below!
    How part? On this keen ridge
But one may pass. They call you—go!
    My life shall be your bridge.

[?] (1909)

Wharton recorded this poem in one of her notebooks. She employs the rhyme scheme of the *quintilla* or Spanish *quintain* in one of her most beautiful fusions of sound, form, and feeling.

🌿

I HAVE had your love and I have seen it go.
And still
There is a glory on the western hill
And I can bear the faces that I know.
I have had your love and I have seen it go.

It was not sorrow that I felt before;
For then
I felt myself an alien among men,
And now I see my face in every door
And hear, o'er head, my pain that walks the floor.

A wind arises and the land is green.
I know
There must be veins that feel the tree sap flow.
I have forgotten what the seasons mean . . .
I have had your love and I have seen it go.

[1913] (2019)

Sometimes bitterness overcame even the consolation of the Psalms (51:8).

🐚 Martyrdom

"The bones that thou has broken shall rejoice"—
False prophecy, O vain and lying voice!
The bones that Love hath broken, never again
Shall hope make whole, nor pleasure ease their pain.

How long the way is that they have to tread,
Whose feet against the thorns of Love have bled,
How blind and wearily they grope, whose eyes
Love's lightning blasted in the morning skies!

What ails all mirth, all virtue, all desire,
To feather and fall like ashes without fire
Beneath the frozen touch of those who try
To find some warmth in life when Love goes by?

Yea, Love hath turned our honour to a ghost,
And nought seems real save that which we have lost,
And not until the grave, O lying voice,
The bones that Love hath broken shall rejoice.

[?] (2019)

The next three poems appear at the end of Wharton's poetry notebook. While most of the notebook can be dated to 1889–93, the last few pages might have been added later. Thus we can only guess when these were written—before or after her affair with Fullerton? The last lines of this poem echo the ending of Wharton's early novel *The House of Mirth*, in which Lily Bart dies with one word unspoken between her and the man who should have loved and saved her.

O LOVE, let the world for once go by,
With its danger-signals and warning cry,
Or else let us dream it was swung in space
Just that we two might stand face to face,
Soul within soul, as eye within eye,
Deaf, blind to all else save the you and the me—
Ah, for once, my life, let the whole world be!
What! We had promised? The words were not ours—
What! There's a heart dead? But ours are just born—

Ay, what will it matter, when all are dead,
That we died apart, with one word unsaid?

[?] (2005)

❧ Two Days

Two days gone since we parted? What, two days
Tumultuous with leashed thoughts that cry aloud
Against the iron silence of the crowd,
Marvels that press upon the full-brimmed gaze,
Bursts of blue summits, echoes of lost lays,
And a god's glimmer through the rifted cloud?
All these were ours, all these we disavowed,
Turning in pride to walk our separate ways.

Though many days together yet shall yield
Their golden harvest to the soul and eye,
Ungleaned forever lies the mystic field
Of these irrevocable days gone by,
And never to us two shall be revealed
The vision of the god who passed so nigh.

[?] (2019)

Avowal

IF only I might say with all my soul
What all my senses in your presence say:
"Come, let us live our life and have our way,
Reject the half, and boldly take the whole,
Believe the world was made for our control,
And put all scruples with all doubts away"—
Yea, had I strength to take a sword and slay
The lives that lie between us, till we sole
Stood face to face in love's high solitude—
Well, and what then? This only, that between
Us and our memory's revengeful brood,
Gorged with the life-blood of the should-have-been,
And flocking fast to seize us for their food,
One moment of full life might intervene.

[?] (2019)

Wharton was sixty-six years old when this poem was published—but we don't know when it was written. The speaker here confronts not only lost love, but old age as well, and worse—the possibility that she was never really loved. There are several Nairas in ancient Greek stories, but the most likely one to which Wharton refers was a woman in her fifties condemned by Apollodorus as a prostitute.

🎵 Had I Been Only

HAD I been only that which you enjoyed,
Nought were I now but old grimacing bones,
Masking with painted lips rheumatic groans,
The spectre of past pleasures that have cloyed,
The blossomed shade where Amaryllis toyed
Turned to a wilderness of stumps and stones,
Or gaunt Næera, among kindred crones,
Superfluous, meddlesome and unemployed.

Best comradeship, how frail a tie it is,
Though we entreat of it its sure delights!
Can any love our days that loved our nights,
Or feign contentment who has fed on bliss?
Not lips alone become too old to kiss;
Yet, O my other soul—was I but this?

[?] (1928)

Arresting Characters

As a fiction writer, Wharton excelled at creating interesting characters and following them in and out of predicaments, often of their own making. In novels and stories, traditionally the writer must construct a plot as well as draw characters. Narrative poems, particularly dramatic monologues, offer a different way in, an opportunity to explore a character's motivation from the interior. Story is revealed in retrospect, in bits and pieces that the reader must put together, and cadence, repetition, and sound add to the drama. A good dramatic monologue reveals more about the speaker than he or she realizes, giving rise to the ironies Wharton was so adept at delineating. As we have seen in other poems, Wharton was fascinated with the distant past, and she used this form to explore various historical, biblical, and mythological figures, often giving new interpretations of familiar figures.

This sonnet—not yet perfected in its form—was written when Wharton was thirteen years old. We can perhaps see Tennyson and Keats at work here, a Romantic view of faith, and an early ability to create a character. Rather than a dramatic monologue, the poem describes the medieval figure from the outside, suggesting her piety by her actions rather than her thoughts.

Vespers

It is the vesper hour, and in yon aisle
Where fainting incense clouds the heavy air
My lady's kneeling at her evening prayer,
Alone and silently; for in a file
The choristers have passed, and left her there,
Where martyrs from the tinted windows stare,
And saints look downward with a holy smile
Upon her meek devotions, while the day
Fades slowly, and a tender amber light
From coloured panes about her head doth play—
Her veil falls like a shade, and ghostly white
Her clasped hands glimmer through the deepening gray;
So will she kneel, until from Heaven's height
The Angels bend to hear their sister pray.

[November 11, 1875] (1879)

Margaret of Cortona

BY EDITH WHARTON

FRA PAOLO, since they say the end is near,
  And you of all men have the gentlest eyes,
  Most like our father Francis; since you know
How I have toiled and prayed and scourged and striven,
Mothered the orphan, waked beside the sick,
Gone empty that mine enemy might eat,
Given bread for stones in famine years, and channelled
With vigilant knees the pavement of this cell,
Till I constrained the Christ upon the wall
To bend His thorn-crowned Head in mute forgiveness . . .
Three times He bowed it . . . (but the whole stands writ,
Sealed with the Bishop's signet, as you know),
Once for each person of the Blessed Three——
A miracle that the whole town attests,
The very babes thrust forward for my blessing,
And either parish plotting for my bones——
Since this you know: sit near and bear with me.

"Margaret of Cortona" as it appeared in *Harper's Magazine*
in 1901, illustrated by Howard Pyle.

Some twenty years after writing "Vespers," Wharton chose another religious woman for an interior exploration of character. Margaret of Cortona was a thirteenth-century Tuscan saint. A willful and reckless girl, at seventeen she ran away with a man and bore his child. After her lover was murdered, she sought refuge in the Church and joined the Order of St. Francis of Assisi. She is said to have been so devout that she heard the voice of Jesus and could commune with him. Here Wharton imagines Saint Margaret on her deathbed, where truth insists on being voiced. Contemporary Catholics were scandalized by what they considered blasphemous and immorally suggestive—an insult to the saint—and *Harper's* felt compelled to issue a public apology.

Margaret of Cortona

FRA PAOLO, since they say the end is near,
And you of all men have the gentlest eyes,
Most like our father Francis; since you know
How I have toiled and prayed and scourged and striven,
Mothered the orphan, waked beside the sick,
Gone empty that mine enemy might eat,
Given bread for stones in famine years, and channelled
With vigilant knees the pavement of this cell,
Till I constrained the Christ upon the wall
To bend His thorn-crowned Head in mute forgiveness . . .
Three times He bowed it . . . (but the whole stands writ,
Sealed with the Bishop's signet, as you know),
Once for each person of the Blessed Three——
A miracle that the whole town attests,
The very babes thrust forward for my blessing,

And either parish plotting for my bones——
Since this you know: sit near and bear with me.

I have lain here, these many empty days
I thought to pack with Credos and Hail Marys
So close that not a fear should force the door——
But still, between the blessed syllables
That taper up like blazing angel heads,
Praise over praise, to the Unutterable,
Strange questions clutch me, thrusting fiery arms,
As though, athwart the close-meshed litanies,
My dead should pluck at me from hell, with eyes
Alive in their obliterated faces! . . .
I have tried the saints' names and our blessed Mother's,
Fra Paolo, I have tried them o'er and o'er,
And like a blade bent backward at first thrust
They yield and fail me—and the questions stay.
And so I thought, into some human heart,
Pure, and yet foot-worn with the tread of sin,
If only I might creep for sanctuary,
It might be that those eyes would let me rest . . .

Fra Paolo, listen. How should I forget
The day I saw him first? (You know the one.)
I had been laughing in the market-place
With others like me, I the youngest there,
Jostling about a pack of mountebanks
Like flies on carrion (I the youngest there!),
Till darkness fell; and while the other girls
Turned this way, that way, as perdition beckoned,

I, wondering what the night would bring, half hoping:
If not, this once, a child's sleep in my garret,
At least enough to buy that two-pronged coral
The others covet 'gainst the evil eye,
Since, after all, one sees that I'm the youngest——
So, muttering my litany to hell
(The only prayer I knew that was not Latin),
Felt on my arm a touch as kind as yours,
And heard a voice as kind as yours say "Come."
I turned and went; and from that day I never
Looked on the face of any other man.
So much is known; so much effaced; the sin
Cast like a plague-struck body to the sea,
Deep, deep into the unfathomable pardon——
(The Head bowed thrice, as the whole town attests).
What more, then? To what purpose? Bear with me!——

It seems that he, a stranger in the place,
First noted me that afternoon and wondered:
How grew so white a bud in such black slime,
And why not mine the hand to pluck it out?
Why, so Christ deals with souls, you cry—what then?
Not so! Not so! When Christ, the heavenly gardener,
Plucks flowers for Paradise (do I not know?),
He snaps the stem above the root, and presses
The ransomed soul between two convent walls,
A lifeless blossom in the Book of Life.
But when my lover gathered me, he lifted
Stem, root and all—ay, and the clinging mud—
And set me on his sill to spread and bloom

After the common way, take sun and rain,
And make a patch of brightness for the street,
Though raised above rough fingers—so you make
A weed a flower, and others, passing, think:
"Next ditch I cross, I'll lift a root from it,
And dress my window" . . . and the blessing spreads.
Well, so I grew, with every root and tendril
Grappling the secret anchorage of his love,
And so we loved each other till he died. . . .

Ah, that black night he left me, that dead dawn
I found him lying in the woods, alive
To gasp my name out and his life-blood with it,
As though the murderer's knife had probed for me
In his hacked breast and found me in each wound . . .
Well, it was there Christ came to me, you know,
And led me home—just as that other led me.
(*Just as that other?* Father, bear with me!)
My lover's death, they tell me, saved my soul,
And I have lived to be a light to men,
And gather sinners to the knees of grace,

All this, you say, the Bishop's signet covers.
But stay! Suppose my lover had not died?
(At last my question! Father, help me face it.)
I say: Suppose my lover had not died—
Think you I ever would have left him living,
Even to be Christ's blessed Margaret?
—We lived in sin? Why, to the sin I died to
That other was a Paradise, when God

Walks there at eventide, the air pure gold,
And angels treading all the grass to flowers!
He was my Christ—he led me out of hell——
He died to save me (so your casuists say!)——
Could Christ do more? Your Christ out-pity mine?
Why, *yours* but let the sinner bathe His feet;
Mine raised her to the level of his heart . . .
And then Christ's way is saving, as man's way
Is squandering—and the devil take the shards!
But this man kept for sacramental use
The cup that once had slaked a passing thirst;
This man declared: "The same clay serves to model
A devil or a saint; the scribe may stain
The same fair parchment with obscenities,
Or gild with benedictions; nay," he cried,
"Because a satyr feasted in this wood,
And fouled the grasses with carousing foot,
Shall not a hermit build his chapel here
And cleanse the echoes with his litanies?
The sodden grasses spring again—why not
The trampled soul? Is man less merciful
Than nature, good more fugitive than grass?"
And so—if, after all, he had not died,
And suddenly that door should know his hand,
And with that voice as kind as yours he said:
"Come, Margaret, forth into the sun again,
Back to the life we fashioned with our hands
Out of old sins and follies, fragments scorned
Of more ambitious builders, yet by Love,
The patient architect, so shaped and fitted

That not a crevice let the winter in—"
Think you my bones would not arise and walk,
This bruisèd body (as once the bruisèd soul)
Turn from the wonders of the seventh heaven
As from the antics of the market-place?
If this could be (as I so oft have dreamed),
I, who have known both loves, divine and human,
Think you I would not leave this Christ for that?

—I rave, you say? You start from me, Fra Paolo?
Go, then; your going leaves me not alone.
I marvel, rather, that I feared the question,
Since, now I name it, it draws near to me
With such dear reassurance in its eyes,
And takes your place beside me . . .
                              Nay, I tell you,
Fra Paolo, I have cried on all the saints—
If this be devil's prompting, let them drown it
In Alleluias! Yet not one replies.
And, for the Christ there—is He silent too?
Your Christ? Poor father; you that have but one,
And that one silent—how I pity you!
He will not answer? Will not help you cast
The devil out? But hangs there on the wall,
Blind wood and bone——?
                              How if *I* call on Him——
I, whom He talks with, as the town attests?
If ever prayer hath ravished me so high
That its wings failed and dropped me in Thy breast,
Christ, I adjure thee! By that naked hour

Of innermost commixture, when my soul
Contained Thee as the paten holds the host,
Judge Thou alone between this priest and me;
Nay, rather, Lord, between my past and present,
Thy Margaret and that other's—whose she is
By right of salvage—and whose call should follow!
Thine? Silent still. —— Or his, who stooped to her,
And drew her to Thee by the bands of love?
Not Thine? Then his?

                Ah, Christ—the thorn-crowned Head
Bends . . . bends again . . . down on your knees, Fra Paolo!
If his, then Thine!

                Kneel, priest, for this is heaven . . .

[?] (1901)

With typical irony, Wharton chooses to name the unfortunate subject of this poem Cynthia, an epithet of Artemis, goddess of the moon, of chastity, and of the hunt. But which way does the irony cut?

🐛 Cynthia

HE found her in the street one night. She said:
"I sin to get my mother's daily bread;
I know no other way; I never learned
To cook or sew"—and deep his anger burned
That the child's shame should feed the mother's mouth,
And so, in pity of her piteous youth,
Her sixteen years made up of bitter nights,
And short days shorn of natural delights,
He took her home. Her pinched and pretty face
Wore, with the passing months, a graver grace,
A light as if of youth won back again
After long stress of peril and of pain,
Regenerate in love's sight. He taught her hands
All that a woman's household skill commands,
Her puzzled eyes to read, her lips to speak
Gentlest words only, and her heart to seek
His trustfully, till she to him became
A daughter, and to hide her cast-off shame
From the world's eye he called her Cynthia Grey,
Child of a friend who, dying far away
In tropic ardours, left the girl to him.
And in the minds of both the past grew dim,
She dazzled with the dawn of hope, and he

Washing her white in pity's boundless sea,
Till both forgot that each of them had been
Led to the other by the hand of sin.

Scarce of this tranquil life five years were sped
When his sole nephew came to him and said,
"I love your friend's child Cynthia; she will be
My wife if you are willing"—whereat he,
To whom the boy was dearer than a son,
Cursed in his heart the deed that he had done,
And, venting his self-anger on the head
He loved the best, with sudden violence said:
"No more of this, for it shall never be,
Though your entreaties storm me like the sea
Storming the shore. Why, there are fairer far
Than she is, for the asking."
                                    "Though there are,"
The nephew answered, "there are none for me.
Save this one woman only, and why not she?"

"Why not? Why not? The girl is scarce of age,
Lacks gold, and has no hope of heritage."

"But I have both," the lover answered, "find
Some better way than that to turn my mind
From loving Cynthia."
                            Then the Uncle said,
"Now for your mother's sake, my sister dead,
Ask me no more. While I have breath of life,
I swear you shall not take the girl to wife!"

"God be my witness that I shall," the lad
Replied half-smiling, and the look he had
Maddened the other, thinking that his race
Should bear the imprint of a harlot's face
In after years, and his dead sister's child
Rear children from a life-spring so defiled
With currents of vile blood without a name,
Fed from a shameless ancestry of shame,
And from his lips the sudden answer broke,
"Since on your head the lightning you invoke,
Listen—I found your Cynthia in the street,
Mixed with the mire that clung about my feet,
And in vain pity, snatched her from the slough,
Washing the mud from her smirched lips and brow;
But what she was, deeper than what she is,
Lives on, red-branded with corruption's kiss."

But still the lover, though his lips had paled,
Stood resolute. "Perchance you had prevailed
Had I not loved her, but Love can still make whole
The broken body and the blasted soul."

"What? Will you shelter with your mother's name
The forehead blazoned with the brand of shame?
What? Will you touch with consecrated love
The lips a hundred lips grew weary of
Ere yours caressed them? Shall your children's eyes
Taunt you with half-suspected prophecies
Of evil, and the patter of their feet
Remind you hers have wandered in the street?"

"Love is a god, and Love can make," he said,
"New heavens and earth, and Love can raise the dead
Face of lost innocence from charnel-caves
Of death and darkness; Love is a pool whose waves
Bring healing to the leprous limbs of sin,
And pure as snow are they that wash therein."

And then the other, for a little space,
Was silent, till the lad's uplifted face
Of visionary triumph stung his pride,
And "Take her then to be your wife," he cried,
"(If even at this your love makes no demur)
Who was my mistress ere I rescued her!"

With lifted hand, as if to fend a blow
Too heavy to be borne, and head bent low,
The lover heard him, all the effluent blood
Back-ebbing to his heart—when there she stood,
Cynthia, her hand upon the door, her face
Paler than his, and for a moment's space
All three were speechless; then the girl began—

"Is there no mercy in the heart of man
That he should joy to trample in the dust
Those whom his brothers' hands have downward thrust?
Yet kinder those that bind us in the mire,
Than these who lead our groping footsteps higher,
Then fling us down—I never asked to be
Dressed in this robe of new-born purity
You mocked me with. God knows, until you came,

Though I went naked, that I felt no shame,
But you have taught me how to blush, and you
Have taught me how to hide my guilt from view,
And wear the mask of virtue, till I dreamed
That I had grown as holy as I seemed,
And now you teach me that the Christ, who died
To wash the world of sin, was crucified
For men, but not for women"—
                            Then the door
Closed on her, and pale and speechless as before
The two men faced each other, till at last
Forth from his Uncle's face the nephew passed.

That evening Cynthia vanished. He who stood
Alone among the ruins of the good
That he had wrought from evil saw, aghast,
His empty life that fluttered in grief's blast
Like a forsaken nest. She came no more,
Nor did he seek her, though his heart was sore
And many a night he dreamed that she had come.
She came no more—but, to his desolate home
As he returned one night with laggard feet,
Shuddering he heard her laughter in the street.

[1889–93] (2005)

As we have seen, Artemis was the Greek goddess of the hunt, of virginity, and of the natural world, and she was twin sister to Apollo. One day the hunter Actæon came upon her bathing, and, before her nymphs could hide her, saw her naked. In punishment, perhaps so that he could never tell what he had seen, she changed him into a stag, and he was hunted and devoured by his own dogs. Wharton here reimagines the story and tells it, in a dramatic monologue, from the viewpoint of the unexpectedly lonely goddess. This is the title poem of her 1909 collection.

🐝 Artemis to Actæon

THOU couldst not look on me and live: so runs
The mortal legend—thou that couldst not live
Nor look on me (so the divine decree)!
That saw'st me in the cloud, the wave, the bough,
The clod commoved with April, and the shapes
Lurking 'twixt lid and eye-ball in the dark.
Mocked I thee not in every guise of life,
Hid in girls' eyes, a naiad in her well,
Wooed through their laughter, and like echo fled,
Luring thee down the primal silences
Where the heart hushes and the flesh is dumb?
Nay, was not I the tide that drew thee out
Relentlessly from the detaining shore,
Forth from the home-lights and the hailing voices,
Forth from the last faint headland's failing line,
Till I enveloped thee from verge to verge
And hid thee in the hollow of my being?
And still, because between us hung the veil,

The myriad-tinted veil of sense, thy feet
Refused their rest, thy hands the gifts of life,
Thy heart its losses, lest some lesser face
Should blur mine image in thine upturned soul
Ere death had stamped it there. This was thy thought.
And mine?
                    The gods, they say, have all: not so!
This have they—flocks on every hill, the blue
Spirals of incense and the amber drip
Of lucid honey-comb on sylvan shrines,
First-chosen weanlings, doves immaculate,
Twin-cooing in the osier-plaited cage,
And ivy-garlands glaucous with the dew:
Man's wealth, man's servitude, but not himself!
And so they pale, for lack of warmth they wane,
Freeze to the marble of their images,
And, pinnacled on man's subserviency,
Through the thick sacrificial haze discern
Unheeding lives and loves, as some cold peak
Through icy mists may enviously descry
Warm vales unzoned to the all-fruitful sun.
So they along an immortality
Of endless-vistaed homage strain their gaze,
If haply some rash votary, empty-urned,
But light of foot, with all-adventuring hand,
Break rank, fling past the people and the priest,
Up the last step, on to the inmost shrine,
And there, the sacred curtain in his clutch,
Drop dead of seeing—while the others prayed!
Yea, this we wait for, this renews us, this

Incarnates us, pale people of your dreams,
Who are but what you make us, wood or stone,
Or cold chryselephantine hung with gems,
Or else the beating purpose of your life,
Your sword, your clay, the note your pipe pursues,
The face that haunts your pillow, or the light
Scarce visible over leagues of labouring sea!
O thus through use to reign again, to drink
The cup of peradventure to the lees,
For one dear instant disimmortalised
In giving immortality!
So dream the gods upon their listless thrones.
Yet sometimes, when the votary appears,
With death-affronting forehead and glad eyes,
Too young, they rather muse, *too frail thou art,*
And shall we rob some girl of saffron veil
And nuptial garland for so slight a thing?
And so to their incurious loves return.

  Not so with thee; for some indeed there are
Who would behold the truth and then return
To pine among the semblances—but I
Divined in thee the questing foot that never
Revisits the cold hearth of yesterday
Or calls achievement home. I from afar
Beheld thee fashioned for one hour's high use,
Nor meant to slake oblivion drop by drop.
Long, long hadst thou inhabited my dreams,
Surprising me as harts surprise a pool,
Stealing to drink at midnight; I divined

Thee rash to reach the heart of life, and lie
Bosom to bosom in occasion's arms.
And said: *Because I love thee thou shalt die!*

For immortality is not to range
Unlimited through vast Olympian days,
Or sit in dull dominion over time;
But this—to drink fate's utmost at a draught,
Nor feel the wine grow stale upon the lip,
To scale the summit of some soaring moment,
Nor know the dulness of the long descent,
To snatch the crown of life and seal it up
Secure forever in the vaults of death!

And this was thine: to lose thyself in me,
Relive in my renewal, and become
The light of other lives, a quenchless torch
Passed on from hand to hand, till men are dust
And the last garland withers from my shrine.

[1902] (1902)

Although Wharton repudiated this poem after it first came out in 1902 (she wrote a letter to her editor admitting the poem "has made me want to hide under the furniture since I've seen it in print" [EW to William Crary Brownell, 6 November 1902, in Lewis and Lewis, *Letters of Edith Wharton* 75]), she nevertheless included it in her volume *Artemis to Actæon*. Judging by her long footnote, she evidently felt the need to explain the historical events surrounding the sixteenth-century scientist Vesalius and justify her version of his story, something she would never again do in her dramatic monologues. By using this form Wharton can reveal Vesalius's complicated mix of pride, ambition, regret, and, ultimately, acceptance.

🐾 Vesalius in Zante*
(1564)

SET wide the window. Let me drink the day.
I loved light ever, light in eye and brain—

---

* Vesalius, the great anatomist, studied at Louvain and Paris, and was called by Venice to the chair of surgery in the University of Padua. He was one of the first physiologists to dissect the human body, and his great work "The Structure of the Human Body" was an open attack on the physiology of Galen. The book excited such violent opposition, not only in the Church but in the University, that in a fit of discouragement he burned his remaining manuscripts and accepted the post of physician at the Court of Charles V, and afterward of his son, Philip II of Spain. This closed his life of free enquiry, for the Inquisition forbade all scientific research, and the dissection of corpses was prohibited in Spain. Vesalius led for many years the life of the rich and successful court physician, but regrets for his past were never wholly extinguished, and in 1561 they were roused afresh by reading of an anatomical treatise by Gabriel Fallopius, his successor in the chair at Padua. From that moment life in Spain became intolerable to Vesalius, and in 1563 he set out for the East. Tradition reports that this journey was a penance to which the Church condemned him for having opened the body of a woman before she was actually dead; but more probably Vesalius, sick of his long servitude, made the pilgrimage a pretext to escape from Spain.

Fallopius had meanwhile died, and the Venetian Senate is said to have offered Vesalius his old chair; but on the way home from Jerusalem he was seized with illness, and died at Zante in 1564.

No tapers mirrored in long palace floors,
Nor dedicated depths of silent aisles,
But just the common dusty wind-blown day
That roofs earth's millions.
                              O, too long I walked
In that thrice-sifted air that princes breathe,
Nor felt the heaven-wide jostling of the winds
And all the ancient outlawry of earth!
Now let me breathe and see.
                              This pilgrimage
They call a penance—let them call it that!
I set my face to the East to shrive my soul
Of mortal sin? So be it. If my blade
Once questioned living flesh, if once I tore
The pages of the Book in opening it,
See what the torn page yielded ere the light
Had paled its buried characters—and judge!

The girl they brought me, pinioned hand and foot
In catalepsy—say I should have known
That trance had not yet darkened into death,
And held my scalpel. Well, suppose I *knew*?
Sum up the facts—her life against her death.
Her life? The scum upon the pools of pleasure
Breeds such by thousands. And her death? Perchance
The obolus to appease the ferrying Shade,
And waft her into immortality.
Think what she purchased with that one heart-flutter
That whispered its deep secret to my blade!
For, just because her bosom fluttered still,

It told me more than many rifled graves;
Because I spoke too soon, she answered me,
Her vain life ripened to this bud of death
As the whole plant is forced into one flower,
All her blank past a scroll on which God wrote
His word of healing—so that the poor flesh,
Which spread death living, died to purchase life!

Ah, no! The sin I sinned was mine, not theirs.
Not *that* they sent me forth to wash away—
None of their tariffed frailties, but a deed
So far beyond their grasp of good or ill
That, set to weigh it in the Church's balance,
Scarce would they know which scale to cast it in.
But I, I know. I sinned against my will,
Myself, my soul—the God within the breast:
Can any penance wash such sacrilege?

When I was young in Venice, years ago,
I walked the hospice with a Spanish monk,
A solitary cloistered in high thoughts,
The great Loyola, whom I reckoned then
A mere refurbisher of faded creeds,
Expert to edge anew the arms of faith,
As who should say, a Galenist, resolved
To hold the walls of dogma against fact,
Experience, insight, his own self, if need be!
Ah, how I pitied him, mine own eyes set
Straight in the level beams of Truth, who groped
In error's old deserted catacombs

And lit his tapers upon empty graves!
Ay, but he held his own, the monk—more man
Than any laurelled cripple of the wars,
Charles's spent shafts; for what he willed he willed,
As those do that forerun the wheels of fate,
Not take their dust—that force the virgin hours,
Hew life into the likeness of themselves
And wrest the stars from their concurrences.
So firm his mould; but mine the ductile soul
That wears the livery of circumstance
And hangs obsequious on its suzerain's eye.
For who rules now? The twilight-flitting monk,
Or I, that took the morning like an Alp?
He held his own, I let mine slip from me,
The birthright that no sovereign can restore;
And so ironic Time beholds us now
Master and slave—he lord of half the earth,
I ousted from my narrow heritage.

For there's the sting! My kingdom knows me not.
Reach me that folio—my usurper's title!
Fallopius reigning, *vice*—nay, not so:
Successor, not usurper. I am dead.
My throne stood empty; he was heir to it.
Ay, but who hewed his kingdom from the waste,
Cleared, inch by inch, the acres for his sowing,
Won back for man that ancient fief o' the Church,
His body? Who flung Galen from his seat,
And founded the great dynasty of truth

In error's central kingdom?
                              Ask men that,
And see their answer: just a wondering stare
To learn things were not always as they are—
The very fight forgotten with the fighter;
Already grows the moss upon my grave!
Ay, and so meet—hold fast to that, Vesalius.
They only, who re-conquer day by day
The inch of ground they camped on over-night,
Have right of foothold on this crowded earth.
I left mine own; he seized it; with it went
My name, my fame, my very self, it seems,
Till I am but the symbol of a man,
The sign-board creaking o'er an empty inn.
He names me—true! *"Oh, give the door its due*
I entered by. Only, I pray you, note,
Had door been none, a shoulder-thrust of mine
Had breached the crazy wall"—he seems to say.
So meet—and yet a word of thanks, of praise,
Of recognition that the clue was found,
Seized, followed, clung to, by some hand now dust—
Had this obscured his quartering of my shield?

How the one weakness stirs again! I thought
I had done with that old thirst for gratitude
That lured me to the desert years ago.
I did my work—and was not that enough?
No; but because the idlers sneered and shrugged,
The envious whispered, the traducers lied,

And friendship doubted where it should have cheered,
I flung aside the unfinished task, sought praise
Outside my soul's esteem, and learned too late
That victory, like God's kingdom, is within.
(Nay, let the folio rest upon my knee.
I do not feel its weight.) Ingratitude?
The hurrying traveller does not ask the name
Of him who points him on his way; and this
Fallopius sits in the mid-heart of me,
Because he keeps his eye upon the goal,
Cuts a straight furrow to the end in view,
Cares not who oped the fountain by the way,
But drinks to draw fresh courage for his journey.
That was the lesson that Ignatius taught—
The one I might have learned from him, but would not—
That we are but stray atoms on the wind,
A dancing transiency of summer eves,
Till we become one with our purpose, merged
In that vast effort of the race which makes
Mortality immortal.
                                    "He that loseth
His life shall find it": so the Scripture runs.
But I so hugged the fleeting self in me,
So loved the lovely perishable hours,
So kissed myself to death upon their lips,
That on one pyre we perished in the end—
A grimmer bonfire than the Church e'er lit!
Yet all was well—or seemed so—till I heard
That younger voice, an echo of my own,
And, like a wanderer turning to his home,

Who finds another on the hearth, and learns,
Half-dazed, that other is his actual self
In name and claim, as the whole parish swears,
So strangely, suddenly, stood dispossessed
Of that same self I had sold all to keep,
A baffled ghost that none would see or hear!
"Vesalius? Who's Vesalius? This Fallopius
It is who dragged the Galen-idol down,
Who rent the veil of flesh and forced a way
Into the secret fortalice of life"—
Yet it was I that bore the brunt of it!

Well, better so! Better awake and live
My last brief moment as the man I was,
Than lapse from life's long lethargy to death
Without one conscious interval. At least
I repossess my past, am once again
No courtier med'cining the whims of kings
In muffled palace-chambers, but the free
Friendless Vesalius, with his back to the wall
And all the world against him. O, for that
Best gift of all, Fallopius, take my thanks—
That, and much more. At first, when Padua wrote:
"Master, Fallopius dead, resume again
The chair even he could not completely fill,
And see what usury age shall take of youth
In honours forfeited"—why, just at first,
I was quite simply credulously glad
To think the old life stood ajar for me,
Like a fond woman's unforgetting heart.

But now that death waylays me—now I know
This isle is the circumference of my days,
And I shall die here in a little while—
So also best, Fallopius!
                              For I see
The gods may give anew, but not restore;
And though I think that, in my chair again,
I might have argued my supplanters wrong
In this or that—this Cesalpinus, say,
With all his hot-foot blundering in the dark,
Fabricius, with his over-cautious clutch
On Galen (systole and diastole
Of Truth's mysterious heart!)—yet, other ways,
It may be that this dying serves the cause.
For Truth stays not to build her monument
For this or that co-operating hand,
But props it with her servants' failures—nay,
Cements its courses with their blood and brains,
A living substance that shall clinch her walls
Against the assaults of time. Already, see,
Her scaffold rises on my hidden toil,
I but the accepted premiss whence must spring
The airy structure of her argument;
Nor could the bricks it rests on serve to build
The crowning finials. I abide her law:
A different substance for a different end—
Content to know I hold the building up;
Though men, agape at dome and pinnacles,
Guess not, the whole must crumble like a dream
But for that buried labour underneath.

Yet, Padua, I had still my word to say!
Let others say it!—Ah, but will they guess
Just the one word—? Nay, Truth is many-tongued.
What one man failed to speak, another finds
Another word for. May not all converge
In some vast utterance, of which you and I,
Fallopius, were but halting syllables?
So knowledge come, no matter how it comes!
No matter whence the light falls, so it fall!
Truth's way, not mine—that I, whose service failed
In action, yet may make amends in praise.
Fabricius, Cesalpinus, say your word,
Not yours, or mine, but Truth's, as you receive it!
You miss a point I saw? See others, then!
Misread my meaning? Yet expound your own!
Obscure one space I cleared? The sky is wide,
And you may yet uncover other stars.
For thus I read the meaning of this end:
There are two ways of spreading light; to be
The candle or the mirror that reflects it.
I let my wick burn out—there yet remains
To spread an answering surface to the flame
That others kindle.

      Turn me in my bed.
The window darkens as the hours swing round;
But yonder, look, the other casement glows!
Let me face westward as my sun goes down.

[1902] (1902)

Fittingly, this marriage poem was the first Wharton published after she became a wife. Ever interested in Italian history, she writes about the Giustiniani family of Venice, who were noted statesmen, men of the church, and men of letters. In 1171, a massacre and subsequent plague killed nearly all the Venetians in Constantinople, including all the Giustiniani men but one. The remaining son, a monk named Niccolò, was released from his vows in order to marry the daughter of the reigning doge and continue the family line. Wharton would have learned this story from the American author and editor William Dean Howells, who lived in one of the Giustiniani family palaces and wrote about them in *Venetian Life* (1866).

🐚 The Last Giustiniani

O WIFE, wife, wife! As if the sacred name
Could weary one with saying! Once again
Laying against my brow your lips' soft flame,
Join with me, Sweetest, in love's new refrain,
Since the whole music of my late-found life
Is that we call each other "husband—wife."

And yet, stand back, and let your cloth of gold
Straighten its sumptuous lines from waist to knee,
And, flowing firmly outward, fold on fold,
Invest your slim young form with majesty
As when, in those calm bridal robes arrayed,
You stood beside me, and I was afraid.

I was afraid—O sweetness, whiteness, youth,
Best gift of God, I feared you! I, indeed,

For whom all womanhood has been, forsooth,
Summed up in the sole Virgin of the Creed,
I thought that day our Lady's self stood there
And bound herself to me with vow and prayer.

Ah, yes, that day. I sat, remember well,
Half-crook'd above a missal, and laid in
The gold-leaf slowly; silence in my cell;
The picture, Satan tempting Christ to sin
Upon the mount's blue, pointed pinnacle,
The world outspread beneath as fair as hell—

When suddenly they summoned me. I stood
Abashed before the Abbot, who reclined
Full-bellied in his chair beneath the rood,
And roseate with having lately dined;
And then—I standing there abashed—he said:
"The house of Giustiniani all lie dead."

It scarcely seemed to touch me (I had led
A grated life so long) that oversea
My kinsmen in their knighthood should lie dead,
Nor that this sudden death should set me free,
Me, the last Giustiniani—well, what then?
A monk!—The Giustiniani had been men.

So when the Abbot said: "The State decrees
That you, the latest scion of the house
Which died in vain for Venice overseas,
Should be exempted from your sacred vows,

And straightway, when you leave this cloistered place,
Take wife, and add new honors to the race,"

I hardly heard him—would have crept again
To the warped missal—but he snatched a sword
And girded me, and all the heart of men
Rushed through me, as he laughed and hailed me lord,
And, with my hand upon the hilt, I cried,
"Viva San Marco!" like my kin who died.

But, straightway, when, a new-made knight, I stood
Beneath the bridal arch, and saw you come,
A certain monkish warping of the blood
Ran up and struck the man's heart in me dumb;
I breathed an Ave to our Lady's grace,
And did not dare to look upon your face.

And when we swept the waters side by side,
With timbrelled gladness clashing on the air,
I trembled at your image in the tide,
And warded off the devil with a prayer,
Still seeming in a golden dream to move
Through fiendish labyrinths of forbidden love.

But when they left us, and we stood alone,
I, the last Giustiniani, face to face
With your unvisioned beauty, made my own
In this, the last strange bridal of our race,
And, looking up at last to meet your eyes,
Saw in their depths the star of love arise,

Ah, then the monk's garb shrivelled from my heart,
And left me man to face your womanhood.
Without a prayer to keep our lips apart
I turned about and kissed you where you stood,
And gathering all the gladness of my life
Into a new-found word, I called you "wife!"

[?] (1889)

This version of the legend of Tristan and Iseult comes from Joseph Bédier's volume (1900), which recounts the story of the knight Tristan and his uncle's wife, Queen Iseult, who unwittingly drank together from the magic cup of love meant to seal the marriage of Iseult to her husband, King Mark. Fated to be together, the couple ran off and sought shelter with the old hermit Ogrin, who took pity on their state and watched over them until the king's men came to reclaim Iseult. In Wharton's tale, their love is sanctioned by the ancient pagan gods, and its purity convinces even the monk that it is sacred. Wharton was exceedingly pleased that Morton Fullerton praised this poem. The epigraph, from Bédier's *Le Roman de Tristan et Iseult*, translates as "You who judge us, do you know what elixir we drank while we were on the sea?"

Ogrin the Hermit

Vous qui nous jugez, savez-vous quel boivre
nous avons bu sur la mer?

OGRIN the Hermit in old age set forth
This tale to them that sought him in the extreme
Ancient grey wood where he and silence housed:

Long years ago, when yet my sight was keen,
My hearing knew the word of wind in bough,
And all the low fore-runners of the storm,
There reached me, where I sat beneath my thatch,
A crash as of tracked quarry in the brake,
And storm-flecked, fugitive, with straining breasts
And backward eyes and hands inseparable,

Tristan and Iseult, swooning at my feet,
Sought hiding from their hunters. Here they lay.

For pity of their great extremity,
Their sin abhorring, yet not them with it,
I nourished, hid, and suffered them to build
Their branchèd hut in sight of this grey cross,
That haply, falling on their guilty sleep,
Its shadow should part them like the blade of God,
And they should shudder at each other's eyes.

So dwelt they in this solitude with me,
And daily, Tristan forth upon the chase,
The tender Iseult sought my door and heard
The words of holiness. Abashed she heard,
Like one in wisdom nurtured from a child,
Yet in whose ears an alien language dwells
Of some far country whence the traveller brings
Magical treasure, and still images
Of gods forgotten, and the scent of groves
That sleep by painted rivers. As I have seen
Oft-times returning pilgrims with the spell
Of these lost lands upon their lids, she moved
Among familiar truths, accustomed sights,
As she to them were strange, not they to her.
And often, reasoning with her, have I felt
Some ancient lore was in her, dimly drawn
From springs of life beyond the four-fold stream
That makes a silver pale to Paradise;

For she was calm as some forsaken god
Who knows not that his power is passed from him,
But sees with trancèd eyes rich pilgrim-trains
In sands the desert blows about his feet.

Abhorring first, I heard her; yet her speech
Warred not with pity, or the contrite heart,
Or hatred of things evil: rather seemed
The utterance of some world where these are not,
And the heart lives in heathen innocence
With earth's innocuous creatures. For she said:
"Love is not, as the shallow adage goes,
A witch's filter, brewed to trick the blood.
The cup we drank of on the flying deck
Was the blue vault of air, the round world's lip,
Brimmed with life's hydromel, and pressed to ours
By myriad hands of wind and sun and sea.
For these are all the cup-bearers of youth,
That bend above it at the board of life,
Solicitous accomplices: there's not
A leaf on bough, a foam-flash on the wave,
So brief and glancing but it serves them too;
No scent the pale rose spends upon the night,
Nor sky-lark's rapture trusted to the blue,
But these, from the remotest tides of air
Brought in mysterious salvage, breathe and sing
In lovers' lips and eyes; and two that drink
Thus onely of the strange commingled cup
Of mortal fortune shall into their blood
Take magic gifts. Upon each others' hearts

They shall surprise the heart-beat of the world,
And feel a sense of life in things inert;
For as love's touch upon the yielded body
Is a diviner's wand, and where it falls
A hidden treasure trembles: so their eyes,
Falling upon the world of clod and brute,
And cold hearts plotting evil, shall discern
The inextinguishable flame of life
That girdles the remotest frame of things
With influences older than the stars."

So spake Iseult; and thus her passion found
Far-flying words, like birds against the sunset
That look on lands we see not. Yet I know
It was not any argument she found,
But that she was, the colour that life took
About her, that thus reasoned in her stead,
Making her like a lifted lantern borne
Through midnight thickets, where the flitting ray
Momently from inscrutable darkness draws
A myriad-veinèd branch, and its shy nest
Quivering with startled life: so moved Iseult.
And all about her this deep solitude
Stirred with responsive motions. Oft I knelt
In night-long vigil while the lovers slept
Under their outlawed thatch, and with long prayers
Sought to disarm the indignant heavens; but lo,
Thus kneeling in the intertidal hour
'Twixt dark and dawning, have mine eyes beheld
How the old gods that hide in these hoar woods,

And were to me but shapings of the air,
And flit and murmur of the breathing trees,
Or slant of moon on pools—how these stole forth,
Grown living presences, yet not of bale,
But innocent-eyed as fawns that come to drink,
Thronging the threshold where the lovers lay,
In service of the great god housed within
Who hides in his breast, beneath his mighty plumes,
The purposes and penalties of life.
Or in yet deeper hours, when all was still,
And the hushed air bowed over them alone,
Such music of the heart as lovers hear,
When close as lips lean, lean the thoughts between—
When the cold world, no more a lonely orb
Circling the unimagined track of Time,
Is like a beating heart within their hands,
A numb bird that they warm, and feel its wings—
Such music have I heard; and through the prayers
Wherewith I sought to shackle their desires,
And bring them humbled to the feet of God,
Caught the loud quiring of the fruitful year,
The leap of springs, the throb of loosened earth,
And the sound of all the streams that seek the sea.

So fell it, that when pity moved their hearts,
And those high lovers, one unto the end,
Bowed to the sundering will, and each his way
Went through a world that could not make them twain,
Knowing that a great vision, passing by,
Had swept mine eye-lids with its fringe of fire,

I, with the wonder of it on my head,
And with the silence of it in my heart,
Forth to Tintagel went by secret ways,
A long lone journey; and from them that loose
Their spicèd bales upon the wharves, and shake
Strange silks to the sun, or covertly unbosom
Rich hoard of pearls and amber, or let drip
Through swarthy fingers links of sinuous gold,
Chose their most delicate treasures. Though I knew
No touch more silken than this knotted gown,
My hands, grown tender with the sense of her,
Discerned the airiest tissues, light to cling
As shower-loosed petals, veils like meadow-smoke,
Fur soft as snow, amber like sun congealed,
Pearls pink as may-buds in an orb of dew;
And laden with these wonders, that to her
Were natural as the vesture of a flower,
Fared home to lay my booty at her feet.

And she, consenting, nor with useless words
Proving my purpose, robed herself therein
To meet her lawful lord; but while she thus
Prisoned the wandering glory of her hair,
Dimmed her bright breast with jewels, and subdued
Her light to those dull splendours, well she knew
The lord that I adorned her thus to meet
Was not Tintagel's shadowy King, but he,
That other lord beneath whose plumy feet
The currents of the seas of life run gold
As from eternal sunrise; well she knew

That when I laid my hands upon her head,
Saying, "Fare forth forgiven," the words I spoke
Were the breathings of his pity, who beholds
How, swept on his inexorable wings
Too far beyond the planetary fires
On the last coasts of darkness, plunged too deep
In light ineffable, the heart amazed
Swoons of its glory, and dropping back to earth
Craves the dim shelter of familiar sounds,
The rain on the roof, the noise of flocks that pass,
And the slow world waking to its daily round. . . .

And thus, as one who speeds a banished queen,
I set her on my mule, and hung about
With royal ornament she went her way;
For meet it was that this great Queen should pass
Crowned and forgiven from the face of Love.

[1908–09] (1909)

In Greek mythology, Phaedra, the wife of King Theseus, falls in love with her stepson Hippolytus. She hides her pursuit of him from her husband by accusing Hippolytus of improper lust (in some versions rape), and so Theseus condemns Hippolytus to death. Phaedra cannot live with her deceit and loss and kills herself. We are meant to understand that Phaedra's actions were fated: she had inherited from her grandfather, Sol, the curse of forbidden desire.

Phaedra

Not that on me the Cyprian fury fell,
    Last martyr of my love-ensanguined race;
    Not that my children drop the averted face
When my name shames the silence; not that hell
Holds me where nevermore his glance shall dwell
    Nightlong between my lids, my pulses race
    Through flying pines the tempest of the chase,
Nor my heart rest with him beside the well.

Not that he hates me; not, O baffled gods—
    Not that I slew him!—yet, because your goal
Is always reached, nor your rejoicing rods
Fell ever yet upon insensate clods,
    Know, the one pang that makes your triumph whole
    Is, that he knows the baseness of my soul.

[?] (1898)

The subject of numerous plays and stories, Lucrezia Malpigli (b. 1572)—Wharton misspells it as "Malvigli"—was married by her family to Lelio Buonvisi (who, despite Wharton's implication, was only six years her senior). Accounts vary as to the status of Lucrezia's relationship with Massimiliano Arnolfini before and during her marriage. In his passion to have her, perhaps with Lucrezia's complicity, Arnolfini murdered Buonvisi. Lucrezia fled to a nunnery for shelter. By all accounts she did not remain chaste, accepting lovers from many of the most powerful families in Lucca. She was later disciplined for sexual incontinence and possibly murder. Arnolfini roamed unpunished for more than twenty years, but ultimately he was imprisoned and went mad. The crime and ensuing feud among the three major families of Lucca caused chaos and blood on the streets for generations. Wharton read about it in John Addington Symonds's *Renaissance in Italy: The Catholic Reaction*, and probably also in an article about Italian women in the Middle Ages in *The Fortnightly Review* (vol. 49, 1888). These two poems tell quite different stories, first from Lucrezia's point of view, then from Arnolfini's. Once again, in the second poem, we encounter the image of lovers parting with crucial words left unsaid.

🐛 Lucrezia Buonvisi Remembers

Ay, trill to your lute that you love me—you that never saw fear
Her head through the flowers of passion like a crested serpent
        rear!
I was always a coward myself—but the best of love that I had
I gave to the man that laughed in the face of fear and was glad.

Long, long ago—you remember—it was town talk when I was
        young,

(For shame is sweeter than honey on many a saintly tongue)
Long, long ago, at the Este's court, we looked in each other's
      eyes
And knew that our hour was coming, whatever the world might
      devise;
Then they gave me to old Buonvisi, and the Luccan palace grey
Held me fast like a fly in amber for many a long dull day,
Till at last (I had known it and waited) we met as I knew we
      should meet
At a ball, with a whispered word—he was master of guile and
      deceit—
And there in the face of Buonvisi we planned to cheat him, I
      say,
And so we did, God's body, for many a long, sweet day,
Till there came a rumour of peril, and my lover smiled and said
"It is time, my flower of red, that the far going fool were dead"—
As a man might say of a fly that had buzzed too long at his head.

But those that are loud with their tongues most often are mute
      with the sword—
Not he! It was always the scabbard that spoke his final word,
And my heart grew big with his purpose as he laid his lips on
      mine,
Vowing next dawn should see us loose rein for the border-line.

That eve, as I walked from vespers, head bent, at Buonvisi's heel
They fell on him thick in the archway and answered his cry with
      steel,
Till he dropped face-downward, dumb (he had prated all his
      life,

It was time he should hold his peace) and I fled like the quarry
      that hears
The bay of the hounds at its throat, for my still-born courage fell
As I thought of Buonvisi's soul gone down to await us in Hell,
And remembered the screws and the pincers, the dungeons
      dripping with slime,
Where women as fair as I have grown old for a moment of
      crime,
Till a madness of terror possessed me, and like Peter denying his
      lord,
I lied to the love in my soul for fear of the rack and the cord.

So I fled to the convent, confessed, bought peace for my soul of
      the Pope,
And lay dumb as a bird in the grass when she knows that the
      fowler's agrope
While he, unsheltered, alone, with the price of my sin on his
      head,
Waited and wondered and scorned me—and now perchance
      lies dead!

[1889–93] (2019)

🎵 Lucrezia Buonvisi's Lover
(Dying at Viareggio)

LEAGUE upon league the long grey line of sea
Girdles this weary coast, and league on league
The grey sky follows it—but I instead
See, sometimes, Lucca, with its sunny streets,
Proud palaces and churches and, beyond,
The vine-linked trees, the meadows and the hills.
There the Buonvisi palace stands. I knew
The night young Lelio brought her home; I stood
And watched the torches flare about his gates
And, through the windows, in a blaze of light,
Satyrs and nymphs that lolled above the cornice;
But I outside among the linkmen laughed
To think those bridal lips young Lelio kissed
Had fluttered under mine; to think he held
Hands, eyes, and brow, and hair's imprisoned light,
His by divine ordainment—ah, we knew
Better than that, Lucrezia, in Ferrara!

Next eve we met at the Malvigli's ball.
I see her now, as up the palace floor
He led her, with her slender head erect
Above his jewels (no one saw the pearls
against her throat), her undulating tread,
Her pure, pale brow, and virginal faint smile,
Reluctant, yet how tender! Then her eyes
That the rude light offends (or so it seems,

So close their blue lids lattice them) as though
The sun, that looks alike on good and evil,
Might cloud such wells of holiness.

                    I bowed,
Falling aside to let her splendour pass;
But he, poor fool, puffed with his pride in her,
Must needs detain me with a boastful word:
"Welcome to Lucca! Pity that you came
A day late for our wedding. Scold him, Sweet."
I thanked him, while a curse beneath my smile
Slept like a dagger in a velvet sheath,
She standing silent, with that way she had
When words might prove misleading. So they passed.

But later, in the contradance, I said
As our hands met: "Lucrezia, you remember
The old days in Ferrara?"

                    I could swear
That, as she curtsied to the ground, I saw
A quiver of the lashes down her cheek.
We crossed, divided, joined again. I said:
"Over against your palace windows stands
A little house one heeds not. One might reach it
At nightfall by the gate upon the lane."

Again we parted; when we met again
She asked, "What might one find there?"

I replied,
"One who so greatly loves that he can wait,
And yet so hotly that to wait is pain.
The house is safe, the weaver's wife, Pollonia,
Who lives there, to be trusted"—

       Then the dance
Ceased, and her partner led her to her seat.

I waited at Pollonia's many a day
Before she came—still the same wise Lucrezia
Who, at Ferrara, from my arms would go
Unflinching to confession; still the same
Who, when her parents bade her wed Buonvisi,
Submitted with a smile. My wise Lucrezia,
I knew that she would come when all was safe,
And so, one eve, the little room was filled
With scent of sandal-wood, and there she stood,
Giving me both her blue-veined hands to kiss,
Yet grudgingly, an eye upon the door
That old Pollonia guarded, half-withdrawn
And listening as in haste to what I said,
With answers flung at random to my prayers,
As mothers silence an importunate child.

Small solace from such meetings could I get.
The palace was too near; and yet the house
Too far for safety; then she feared her husband
The place was full of spies—nay, she had cause
To think her maid was bought—her household duties

Claimed all her care—impossible to say
When she might come again; and still she came,
Watching the hunger that she would not sate,
As children tease some creature through a cage . . .

But once, when I had waited overlong,
And the shame stung me, suddenly I spoke.—
"Sweet, say farewell, and make an end. I ride
Tomorrow to Ferrara. I shall see
That dove-and-serpent face of yours no more
This side the grave, God helping me."

           She said
Nothing at first, but laid her hand in mine
Beseechingly, and made her pleading eyes
Speak her entreaties, till she saw that mine
Were masked with resolution—then she moaned
"Is there no other way?" As a child might,
Lost in a woodland where the branches meet.

I looked upon her once before I answered,
Wondering if that sweet face of hers would shrink;
Then, "The long lane that runs beneath your walls
(The way you go to church) is dark," I said,
"On brightest days; you and your husband go
That way to vespers daily; further on
It bounds a convent-garden, desolate.
Have you not thought, your husband's enemies,
Knowing he goes unarmed and unattended,

Might fall on him some day and strike him down
In that lone stretch along the convent wall?"

Lucrezia, playing with her pearls, was mute;
Then, with a smile she said, "We go to vespers
To-morrow." So great sins, when first they beckon,
Smile and speak childishly to lull our fears.

Thus the next nightfall came. All day it rained,
And thunder rolled about the setting sun.
In the dim church where the Buonvisi pray
Lucrezia, at her Lelio's side, at vespers
Knelt like some saint of Civitali's, carved
Upon a tomb (methought, her husband's tomb),
And when they rose I saw him take her missal,
And with that smile she thanked him.

                  To the street
I stole where, gathered in the cloaking dusk,
My men awaited me. High overhead,
Between the palace-roofs, the narrow sky
Bled with the parting arrows of the sun—
All else was shadow.

                  In the heart I struck him.
He died before the other daggers reached him—
That, I was glad of afterwards—but I,
As through the darkness like a hunted hare
By winding ways well known to me I fled,
And gained the gates, heard always that low cry

She gave—too low to be a cry of warning,
Yet loud enough to soothe his dying ear.

That night I lay in an old house we had,
Muffled in ilexes, beyond the gates;
Then, ere the dawn, to horse; but not before
A messenger whom I could trust, to Lucca
Sped with this message on his breathless lips—
"Meet me, Lucrezia, mine, beyond the border,
My friend shall tell you where; his words are mine."

So gained we Garfagnano. There I waited
And there, she came not! But the messenger
Returned one day, and feared to see my face,
And, when my men compelled him to my feet,
Stammered, "Alas, I bring no answer back."

"Traitor, you lie!"

                          "Messer, I found the lady
Sitting aloof blackrobed among her maids
In the great palace-chamber where Jove woos
Europa on the ceiling. Left alone,
She signed me to approach her. With a smile
She listened to your message; then she took
A purse she had upon her girdle, laid it
Still smiling in my hand, and bade me go.
Next day as at the palace-door I lurked,
Hoping a word, news came to me the lady
Had fled to Santa Chiara in the night.

I followed to the convent; at the door
The portress, tutored to her task, declared:
"Monna Lucrezia on this threshold left
Names, titles, honours. Tell her friends who seek her
Sister Umilia fills her place today
And washes out the bloody past with prayer."

I did not kill the messenger. I laughed,
So true his picture was! Could I not see her
Smile and say nothing, knowing she was safe?

More news came afterwards. She had been warned
To seek the convent's shelter ere her limbs
Followed Pollonia's on the rack. For me
A price was on my head—Some knave betrayed us.
And yet, methinks she might have come to me;
Braving the peril I affronted first,
To reconcile me with a kiss to God!

Well, well, she came not, and the years went by.
I scorned their gifts, yet seized them, as men will,
Reviling what they fight for. All the while
Lucca kept calling me, and as a priest
Carries the Host high o'er a noisome street
So through my life, above its sins and brawls,
I carried my Lucrezia.

Now to make
The story short. A moment came at last
When other loves and other murders, piled

Over the grave of that old crime of ours,
Effaced it from men's memories, and I said:
"Who were the wiser if through Lucca's gates
The outlawed Arnolfini steal once more
And knock at Santa Chiara? It may be
That I shall look upon her face again,
And all the past be paid for."

                    I assumed
A pedlar's guise, gained Lucca, found the means
To show my pretty baubles (gems and rings)
To Santa Chiara's fat confessor. He
Had uses for such trifles, so it seemed,
And then my store of foreign gossip pleased him;
So we waxed friendly over his good wine,
In the green pergola behind the house.

Still I set watch upon my tongue. At last
One stifling day when heavily the bees
Droned from the lilies to the lavender
Across the close-walled garden, I essayed
The question that consumed me: "What of one
The world once called Lucrezia Buonvisi?"

"Sister Umilia? What of her? No good,"
He grumbled, pushing his full glass away
As though the name had soured it.

                    "Is she dead?"
"Dead? No."

                    "Then, Father, if an old, old friend—
A cousin—sued to see her—did you say
You thought I held that amethyst too high?
Yet look how tenderly the waves enwrap
Emergent Thetis! Never mind the waves,
I yield it at your price if I may see her,
Once, only once—look, here's your amethyst."

But with a scowl he put it back. "The nun
You speak of is sequestered. None may see her.
Her comrades dare not look upon her face.
Her food is thrust to her at night—her eyes
This twelve month have not seen the blessed sun."

All the hot garden reeled about my head.
"What was her sin, great God?"

                    "She had a lover."

"A lover? Yes—I know she had a lover,"
I stammered, groping to make clear his words,
"But is that old tale of the Arnolfini
Remembered still against her? Sir, she was
More sinned against than sinning"—

                    Then I saw
His stare upon me. "Ah, you mean the scandal
That sent her here? Ay, that was long ago,
And happened in the world. The Church condoned it.
But this I speak of—this last lover—well,

Best bluntly say, these lovers, since she's had
Enough of them to set the town a-blush,
Passari, Dali, Samminiati"—

                    Nay,
I will not think upon the other names—
I fled from Lucca. All the weary way
That pleading face of hers was at my side—
Thou white corruption, ever at my side!
Shall not death cover up mine eyes from thee?

Well, I am glad that I am dying now,
Though something has escaped me to the end,
One hour I meant to live is still unlived,
One word I meant to say to her unsaid.

What was that word? Of pity, rage, or scorn?
I know not now. Nothing today seems real
But love, and our first kisses at Ferrara. . . .

Lucrezia, my Lucrezia! Still you stand
With the pure brow and virginal faint smile,
Too proud for vindication. God shall judge.

[1889–93] (2019)

In medieval Europe, Church law condemned people with leprosy to be separated from the community and confined to asylums, of which there were some nineteen thousand across Europe, most attended by monks or nuns. Separation was initiated by performing a funeral mass and symbolic burial before banishing the sick to these leper colonies, one of which was in Canterbury. This poem, told from the point of view of a man with leprosy, begins with such a ceremony and ends with his actual death many years later.

The Leper's Funeral and Death
(In mediaeval England)

I

DEAD? Am I dead? These lights against my feet,
The bier I lie on, these my folded hands
Weighed with the cross, the slow funereal chant,
The sable altar and the silent aisles,
All these are death's—but do the dead behold
The faces of their mourners? Do they hear
The sobs drawn inward, count the tears a-quiver
On bended lids, note the poor hands that grope
One for another, as though the living feared
To lose each other in the grasp of death?
Am I not living, and with thrice their life,
I whom the Church calls dead? Nay, dead indeed,
However the heart be throbbing in my throat
Louder than all their sobs, nay dead indeed,
I who now look my last upon my kin,

Who, borne beneath the lych-gate on my bier,
Shall rise from it within the lazar's walls,
To tread the lazar's floor until I die.

There stands the girl I loved—Kate, it was Maytime,
May in the bloom-brimmed hedges and the sky,
That day I kissed you by the hollow oak
That parts the crossways—how the wench is crying,
But she'll forget, come Mayday; you'll forget,
Kate, when young Dickon whistles past the door.
My father's lips are quiet; so he stood
The day they brought our youngest brother home
When the mare trampled him; poor rough grey head,
Bowed with much stooping over children's graves,
This day shall bend thee lower than the rest—
And there, with all his moon-face murked with tears,
There's the lad Tom, God bless him, close to mother—

I will not look upon my mother's face,
Lest I behold its anguish till I die—
I'll shut mine eyes, shut all the weeping out,
And dream that I'm abroad i' the world again,
The kindly world that laughs about our feet
On dewy mornings when we seek the fields,
The pleasant world, full of good neighbours' greetings,
And noisy quips around the tavern door;
And little idle things one wots not of
Till life be over—oh, the blessed world,
Full of light feet that hasten to and fro,
Crossing the thresholds I shall cross no more,

Can there be any sorrow in the world
Like the sorrow of thus leaving it?
Yea, these are sad; but when the thing is over
And they go hence, why, they will laugh again—
Even mother will, at some loud jest of Tom's,
Before the snow is melted from the moor—
And when they die they'll die, and when they're buried
They will become a part of the warm earth,
Not plague-struck ghosts locked in a charnel-house—
And I, the leper, may outlive them all.

II

Now I am dying. How I cried on death
To take me when I left the world behind!
Well, that was idle—life is not so poor,
Even at her basest, but a man will cling
Close-armed about her if she turn from him,
And every day has pleasures, be it only
The smoking porridge brought to us at noon,
The patch of sun to bask in or, in Winter,
The rosy ingle—and when blindness comes,
Why, one can hear the others talking still,
One still can count the footsteps in the court,
And smell the porringers a long way off.

How many years gone since they brought me here?
I know not now—I lose all count of days—
But news comes sometimes from beyond the gates,
Even from the blessèd world that buried us,

And so I know of others that have fared,
For all their hopes, less happily than I.
Kate married Dickon—but that year she died;
And the lad Tom, that went to sea, was drowned;
Thereafter father lay a-bed, they say,
Till in the Spring God took him—last of all
They laid the worn old mother in her grave.
So those my mourners, those that left me here,
Returning to the pleasant ways of men,
To wed and work, and have their fill of life
And love and laughter, and the ease of age,
All, all forgetful of my living death,
Themselves are grown a part of the cold earth,
And I, the leper, have outlived them all.

[1889–93] (2019)

Wharton here reimagines the story of the house of Agamemnon: his sacrifice of his daughter Iphigenia in order to release his fleet for battle; his unfaithful and murderous wife, Clytemnestra; and their son fated to revenge his father's death. Each character is revealed in its own sonnet, a remarkable compression of mythic forces.

🐚 The Oresteia

I

IPHIGENIA.
So brief a way her life went—scarcely more
Than this brief path from palace gate to beach
She ran so often, darting forth to reach
Her father's homing chariot-wheel before
Her elders gained on her; and then such store
Of kisses! Sometimes too a rosy peach
Or white fig from his bosom—one for each,
But hers the roundest, ripest the tree bore.

That tree had first borne blossoms; but in spring
Came a cold storm that rent it, root and top.
Some sheltered blossoms still formed strength to cling,
And these turned fruit; but some were doomed to drop.
The tree spreads upward, widens ring on ring,
And, flushed with fruit, forgets her ruined crop.

II

Agamemnon.
Day drops: the waters whiten to the breeze.
Go forth, glad prows: the Trojan ramparts wait.
Not vainly do ye sail that sail so late,
Quelling at last the indomitable seas.
Yet once, before receding Argos flees,
And morning opes an unimagined gate,
Look back—the pyre that turned the wind of fate
Still smoulders, fanned by the Eumenides.

Go forth: life calls you with the deep's loud cry;
Take ship, O hero, with the favouring gale;
Hushed lies the breast that bled to fill your sail,
And no avenging goddess hovers nigh—
But in your house, laying your raiment by,
Your Queen, unwitting, folds the fatal veil.

III

Clytemnestra.
In this long vigil I grow blind and old.
Watcher, it boots not that I climb with thee
The rampart stairs, and scan the unanswering sea.
Morning and night two faces I behold,
Two faces only, one alive and bold,
The other dead and white. Both follow me,
And one laughs: "Loving, it is bliss to be—"
And one weeps: "Mother, warm me—I am cold."

How should I warm thee, that am cold as thou?
But when across the night the Signals flare
And in the offing looms the fated prow,
Such fiery lust of life in me shall swell
That there'l't leap in me, and my soul shall bear
A terrible brood to sister thee in hell.

IV

Orestes.
This is the fatal veil they trapped him in,
His blood still mingling with its royal hue.
Shall theirs its faded splendour not renew,
And can the all-seeing gods dispute their sin? . . .
The world seems more as once it might have been,
Before my unescapable doom I knew,
And by my sheep-cotes, all the long nights through,
Sharpened my soul until its edge was thin . . .

Is this the roof that sheltered me? There swell
The figs against the wall . . . such little things!
How strange it is the palaces of Kings
Should look like homes where harmless people dwell . . .
Far down the wind I hear the hum of hell,
And in my brain the clang of iron wings.

[?] (2019)

According to the Hebrew Bible, Esther was a beautiful young Jewish woman living in exile in the 400s BCE, part of the harem of the Persian king Ahasuerus, later becoming his queen. The king was unaware that she was Jewish. The king's chief adviser, Haman, swore to destroy the Jews because one of their leaders, Mordechai, refused to bow down to him. But Mordechai was Esther's uncle, and he went to her and entreated her to save her people. Risking her own death, Esther arranged to beguile the king into doing her will, thus saving her people. In Jewish tradition, Haman is the epitome of evil and Esther is a great hero. Wharton, using the traditional hexameter of Latin and Greek epic poetry, here imagines a very different motive for Esther's actions, recalling her so-called blasphemous treatment of Margaret of Cortona.

🐚 Esther

WHEN the news came, and I said, "It is death to go in to the
     King,
Yea, what am I to affront him—his creature, his chattel, his
     thing?"
Then they replied, with the message that Mordecai laid on their
     lips,
"Yea, what art thou to lie safe when thy people shall perish like
     ships,
Ships that the storm overpowereth, black with the burden of
     death,
Scattering their might to the sea to be sucked by its terrible
     breath?
How shalt thou answer, O Esther, to God who hath charged
     thee with these,

If, when the tempest hath fallen, thou ridest alone on the seas?
Get then thy purple upon thee, and spare not the pearls for thy
     hair,
No, nor the gold for thy throat, nor the scent of the sandal-wood
     spare;
Go to the innermost court, where the great King is sitting alone
(Over against him the gateway) aloft on his gold-pillared throne,
Tell him the evil that Haman hath planned in his bosom, yea, give
Boldly his name to the King, who hath said 'there shall none of
     them live'?"
Then a thought stung me, and straightway I smiled as I lifted
     my head.
"Yea, I will go to the King. If I perish I perish," I said.

There in the innermost court, that is curtained with scarlet and
     gold,
Paven with marble, and bounded by walls where his servants
     behold,
Wrought in fair colours, the battles the King in his prowess hath
     won,
There on his throne sat the King, as alone and aloft as the sun;
Yet, as I lifted mine eyes, I beheld in his own my reprieve,
Saw how he reached me the sceptre that bade me approach him
     and live.
"E'en to the half of my kingdom, demand what thou cravest," he
     said,
And I, (with that thought in my heart) as my lips on the sceptre
     I laid,
Answered, "O King, live forever. Thy handmaid entreats thee to
     come,

Thou, and Prince Haman thy servant, tonight to the doors of
    her home,
There of the banquet to taste that the hand of thy slave hath
    prepared."
"Queen, be it done as thou willest it," gravely the great King
    declared.

Then did they bring me the tunic of purple, the pearls for my
    hair,
Gold of the isles for my girdle, and spices to sweeten the air;
So in my doorway I stood, and awaited the will of my lord.
With him came Haman the Prince, and they entered and sat at
    the board.
Deep drank the King, but that other sat silent and watched me,
    and I
Knew that his eyes held my beauty, as pools hold a fragment of
    sky.
So I was patient, and waited; and when the King rose it was
    light.
"Ask what thou willest," he bade me; and, "come to thy hand-
    maid tonight,
Thou, and Prince Haman thy servant, to taste of the wine-cup,"
    I said;
"So shall it be," swore the King, "by the pearl-woven hairs of
    thy head."

Then I made ready again, and awaited the King and his friend,
But to myself in my soul I said, "coward, tonight it shall end."
So, when the goblets of gold, with the vine-woven bordering,
    swung

High overhead, like strange fruits on a wind-stricken orchard-
　　　bough hung,
Swaying now this way, now that, in a passionate mid-summer
　　　gale,
When, as I leaned on my pillows, I marked through a rift of my
　　　veil
Hot in the eyes of my master the fumes of the wine-cup arise,
Like to the dust of a chariot clouding a foot-runner's eyes,
Then from the gold-carven couch at his side I arose with a
　　　spring,
Crying out, "Mercy, O Master," and crying out, "Vengeance, O
　　　King!
Lo, we are sold to destruction, yea, sold to the edge of the
　　　sword,
I and my people are sold to the hand of our enemies, Lord.
Save us, O mighty to conquer! My voice is the voice of their
　　　prayers;
Lord, if my people must perish, my doom shall be even as theirs."

Down with a crash the King's goblet fell—forth, like a torrent of
　　　blood,
Red betwixt Haman and me, poured the wine in an ominous
　　　flood—
"Give me his name," cried the King, "who hath dared to make
　　　light of my trust;
He that would trample thy people himself shall be trampled like
　　　dust.
Quick, the slave's name!"
　　　　　　　Like a cry in a nightmare my utterance
　　died—

Then, with stretched arm towards Haman, "Behold him, the
          traitor," I cried.
Silent they stood—I could hear the hoarse breath of the two—
          till at last
Forth through the gates of the garden the King in the darkness
          aghast
Fled—
               Then I turned, and, "O foe of my people," I said,
"Here on the breast that betrayed thee let fall for an instant thy
          head.
Give me, O Haman, thy lips. I will pay thee with kisses for
          breath,
Yea, I will pay thee with love for the life I have yielded to death.
Knowest thou now how I love thee? Behold, when the messen-
          ger came,
Clamouring, "Save us, O Queen, from the hate that consumeth
          like flame,"
Thinkst thou I thought of my people? Nay, stood I not safe in
          my place?
But if at last (was my thought) I might speak with him, look on
          his face,
Hold him close-locked to the bosom that thrilled not to pillow a
          King,
Well, though he perished thereby, would he curse me for doing
          this thing?"

Nothing he answered, but only I felt by the lips that he laid
Speechless on mine, that for dying the least of my kisses had paid.
Then the King entered—his face had grown whiter than death
          is with hate—

"What? Shall this slave, this accursèd, lay hands on my Queen?
        Could he wait
Not for one instant my vengeance? O thou that hast vanquished
        him, say,
How shall I deal with the traitor?"
                And smiling I answered him, "Slay."

[?] (2019)

We see here some of the wisdom of Wharton's early observations about women and their necessarily passive lives as they wait for men. Certainly Penelope, wife of Ulysses, is a prototype for the patient wife. Numerous women have written poems retelling *The Odyssey* from Penelope's point of view—Edna St. Vincent Millay, Louise Glück, Dorothy Parker, Margaret Atwood—but Wharton was one of the first.

❦ Penelope

WHAT sacrifice, Ulysses, shall I yield
To win thee back from the unquiet sea,
For whose tumultuous breast thou hast forsaken
The steadfast bosom of thy wife and Queen?
Behold each day when first the dawn begins
To widen o'er the waters, I arise
From my unsharèd couch, and sit me down
Alone beside the window, seaward-turned,
Watching the sails that cross the rippled plain,
If haply one be thine and bear thee home.
But many months unwearied have I watched
The equal rolling of the foam-fringed blue,
I have beheld it dimpling in the sun,
And flaked with snowy birds that dip and fly
That pasture in those upper fields of heaven,
And sheeplike haste before the driving wind,
And I have seen the stormy-crested flood
Arise and battle with whirlwinds might,
Or rocking softly on its soothed breast
The untroubled image of the Summer moon,

As some great mother rocks her sleeping child;
And I, as that same mother might have watched
The everchanging features of her child
Have watched the sea in all its shifting moods
Of peace and storm, until I know it well.
And many sails have I beheld, that rise
And pass and vanish, NONE HATH TARRIED YET.
The tawny sails of fishing-boats at dawn
That put forth from our own indented isle,
And further still, the sails of merchantmen,
And distant farcs o'er the watery roads,
All these have I beheld with wistful eyes,
Pass like the sudden smiles upon a face,
That fading, leave it meaningless and pale—
But thee mine eyes behold not, and in vain
Have I besought the everliving gods
To yield thee back to my unwearied prayer,
For fathomless are their dealings with mankind.

Perchance, indeed, thy prow shall touch no more
The rocky edge of thy deserted home;
It may be, in some dim, enchanted isle
A sorceress hath bound thee to her side,
Or storms have tost thee on some burning coast,
Where, slaving under a barbarian King
Thy life wears downward to a shameful grave,
Perchance thou liest under the great sea
While many ships pass o'er thy sleeping head
And thine uneasy spirit roams the halls
Of death as here it roamed the happy earth.

Or else thy ship hath gained the happy isles
Which often, musing thou hast thought to see
At sunset floating in a golden space
'Twixt sea and sky; and now thou feastest there
With crowned brows, and songs upon thy lips.

But wheresoe'er thy wandering bark is led,
But little thinks thou of the faithful wife,
Who seaward sits and waits for thy return,
For thou wert never cast in lover's mould,
And men at best have much to wean their hearts
From home, and from the fireside's placid joys.
Theirs are the schemes of warfare and adventure
And toiling voyages upon the sea,
Building of ships, and law, and merchandise,
All these are theirs; while in their empty homes
The women sit, and muse upon their love,
And wear their heart with waiting and their eyes
With gazing o'er the irresponsive sea.

[?] (2019)

The Art of Poetry

This section comprises two related groups of poems: poems about poetry—Wharton's own and that of others—and poems about works of visual art. Wharton appreciated craft in words, of course, and also in painting, sculpture, architecture, and other handmade objects. She was a lover of beauty with a sympathetic susceptibility to layers of meaning. As we have seen in earlier poems, she resonated to historical events, mythology, and human emotions and motivation. In writing poems about works of art, called ekphrastic poetry, she joined many poets of her time.

The sonnet was one of Wharton's favorite genres, with its strict rules for meter and rhyme and its invitation to turn an argument. She was not quite the amateur sonneteer she claims to be in this 1891 poem; she had published the accomplished "St. Martin's Summer" ten years earlier. But this one aims high: Petrarch, Shakespeare (whose name she spells in its variant form), and Shelley were all masters of the sonnet. The next three poems show Wharton directly addressing the form.

🐚 The Sonnet

PURE form, that like some chalice of old time
    Contain'st the liquid of the poet's thought
    Within thy curving hollow, gem-enwrought
    With interwoven traceries of rhyme,
While o'er thy brim the bubbling fancies climb,
    What thing am I, that undismayed have sought
    To pour my verse with trembling hand untaught
    Into a shape so small yet so sublime?
Because perfection haunts the hearts of men,
    Because thy sacred chalice gathered up
    The wine of Petrarch, Shakspere, Shelley—then
Receive these tears of failure as they drop
    (Sole vintage of my life), since I am fain
    To pour them in a consecrated cup.

[?] (1891)

𝕮 The Sonnet's Boundaries

I WOULD not have thee widen thy demesne,
Thou garden of the poets, where they stray
When weary with the epic's Alpine way,
Or breathless from the lyric's flight, serene
As some great monarch, who might dreaming lean
From close-railed balcony at set of day,
And tranquilly his outspread realm survey,
Or muse on what his conquests might have been.

Through lily and rose of alternating rhyme
Thy sinuous windings lead the spirit on;
No floods to cross, no peaks are here to climb,
Yet here the wariest wanderer were undone
If, onward lured by thy recurrent chime,
Thy magic boundaries he should overrun.

[1889–93] (2019)

🐚 A Vision

ON the wide shores of melody I strayed
One amber dawn when from the waves arose
The form of one white-vested, girdled close,
Who lightly lifted up her radiant head,
So that her bosom's tranquil curve displayed
A necklet where, in alternating rows,
Four jewels caught the sunrise. Windless snows
Fall not as soft as her unsounding tread.

Straight to my side she came, with eyes benign,
Swift as a creature borne upon the wing,
And, gazing breathless on her face divine,
Lit with a smile elusive as the Spring,
I heard her murmur in a voice like mine,
"I am the Sonnet thou hast tried to sing!"

[1889–93] (2019)

As birds from some green tropic gloom,
By homeless seas & blinding sands,
Wing onward to an unknown doom
In unimagined northern lands,

Trusting, as day & night they fare
Across the rolling world's unrest,
There buds in some far April air
The tendril curved to hold their nest;

O'er painted deserts mocked with light,
And shores where bitter surges roll,
Year after year these songs took flight
From hidden coverts of the soul.

No instinct of unvisioned springs
Upheld them with the hope of rest—
Yet let them fold their happy wings
One wondering moment in your breast.

April 23: 1909.

Facsimile of "[As birds from some green tropic gloom]," hand-inscribed by Wharton to her lover Morton Fullerton in his presentation copy of *Artemis to Actæon*.

Here we have a much more intimate poem. Wharton inscribed it on the flyleaf of the copy of *Artemis to Actæon* that she gave to Morton Fullerton, dated April 23, 1909. It discloses her passionate wish to be heard and understood and implies that Wharton had used poetry all of her life to express her innermost feelings, yearning for a sympathetic listener. Sad indeed to find that Fullerton's copy was hardly opened; only "The Mortal Lease," the poem she wrote for him, seems to have been read.

As birds from some green tropic gloom,
By homeless seas and blinding sands,
Wing onward to an unknown doom
In unimagined northern lands,

Trusting, as day and night they fare
Across the rolling world's unrest,
There buds in some far April air
The tendril curved to hold their nest;

O'er painted deserts mocked with light,
And shores where bitter surges roll,
Year after year these songs took flight
From hidden coverts of the soul.

No instinct of unvisioned springs
Upheld them with the hope of rest—
Yet let them fold their happy wings
One wondering moment in your breast.

[1909] (2019)

Turning to other writers, Wharton expressed her appreciation—and perhaps her exasperation—for their work as well. One of her great loves was Dante's *Inferno*, which she struggled over several times in the original Italian. In 1889 she wrote to her former governess, Anna Bahlmann:

I am reading the Inferno. It is rather hard work, as I have to use Longfellow's translation as a help, & I have never before got beyond 10 or 12 Cantos, but this time I am well on in the teens, & much absorbed of course. What images! I have ghosts who eye Dante as men "look at one another sharply at night, beneath the new moon"—the whirlwind that goes on its way "superb & powderous" (This word is mine, Longfellow calls it "laden with dust" or something of that sort) & that magnificent rebuke—

"No martyrdom, save that of thine own rage
Were for thy rage sufficient martyrdom"

Longfellow's translation is perfectly unpoetic & perfectly literal, therefore most useful & not distracting. And then the piercing sweetness of such lines as "Guardami ben, ben son, ben son, Beatrice"—Well, I am almost afraid it is finer than Milton—& what would it be to any one who really knew Italian well!—

Wharton was referring to the moment in *Purgatorio* when Dante finally sees Beatrice. John Ciardi translates the line as "Look at me well. I am she. I am Beatrice" (XXX, 73). *"Perchè mi schiante"*: "Why are you tearing me?" (XIII, 33, Ciardi).

The Inferno

AND didst thou see it, Dante? Didst thou see,
Like snow upon a windless Alp, the fall
Of flaming flakes? And didst thou hear the call,
"Perchè mi schiante?" of the tortured tree,
And look upon the faces of the three
Who stayed thee near the torrent's blinding brawl?
Master, I know thou sawst and heardst it all,
As I, who read thy pages, hear and see.

So lead me through the kingdom of the dead,
Whose awful gateway at thy voice unbars
(As thou wert by the mighty Mantuan led
O'er black precipitous ways and pathless scars)
That I, re-issuing from that fatal shade
Serenely sad, once more may see the stars.

[1889–93] (2019)

Dante

As one who, watching from a lonely height
The rhythmic march of each familiar star,
Sees a new planet swim upon his sight,
Wheeling aloft its flame-encircled car,
And nimbussed with a more transcendent light
Than any of its radiant fellows are,

Thus, Dante, searching with the spirit's gaze
Through the illumined concourse of thy peers,
Aloft among them all I see thee blaze,
And an insufferable splendour sears
My straining eyesight, while the rival rays
Pale and commingle, yielding thee the spheres.

Unmindful of the multitudinous eyes
That burn beneath thy lambent majesty,
I dream that I alone have seen thee rise,
And, wondering that the ignorant world should be
Still locked in darkness, "Wake!" my spirit cries,
"And see the star that God has lit for me!"

[1889–93] (2019)

Here we have Wharton's tribute to Shelley, written after visiting his grave in Rome. The phrase "cor cordium," heart of hearts, is engraved on his tomb at the Protestant cemetery there. Shelley drowned in the Gulf of Spezia and was cremated on the beach at Viareggio, but his heart did not burn; it was preserved by his wife, Mary, and, at her death, interred in St. Peter's Churchyard, Bournemouth, England. As a young teenager Wharton received from her parents a gift of the great Buxton Forman edition of Shelley and she wrote: "Then the gates of the realms of gold swung wide, and from that day to this I don't believe I was ever again, in my inmost self, wholly lonely or unhappy" (*A Backward Glance* 71). Images in this poem recall "Adonais," Shelley's elegy for Keats, as well as "The Cloud" and "Ode to the West Wind."

Cor Cordium

I CAME, O heart of hearts, but not to sing
Where mightiest lips are mute; one April day
When, like a pearl dissolved in light, Rome lay
Clasped in the throbbing hollow of the noon,
I came to pluck one pale anemone
From the green turf that covered thee too soon,
Since lovelier far than earth-born buds must be
The veinèd flowers that from thy life-blood spring.

Long, long I lay, and saw the Roman's tomb
Extend its deepening shadow to the East,
Till suddenly the pomp of sunlight ceased;
Day dropped like a dead warbler from the sky,
And over the shut flowers and songless trees

That watch above the grave of melody,
Like a great vulture borne adoun the breeze
Night swept as suddenly with full-fledged plume.

Flowerlike mine ear upon thy grave took root,
Straining to hear thy beating through the ground,
When the starred silence shook with mighty sound,
Such as the desert's lone ecstatic hears,
Quiring of throats invisible, that seemed
To loosen all the music of the spheres,
As though all loveliness that flashed or beamed
To melody its radiance should transmute.

"Not there," the voices sang, "beneath the sod
The quenchless heart of Shelley beats like flame;
But one with the great heart from whence it came
It pulses through the universe, and thrills
In the wind's whisper to the listening trees,
And the storm's challenge to the startled hills;
It springs at dawn from cloud-built palaces
And walks upon the water like a god.

"Go forth, and give to the revolving year
Thy chainèd spirit, as a maiden frees
Her prisoned songster to the homeless breeze;
Let the stars be to thee like lover's eyes,
When soul sees soul in sacramental hour,
Closer than lover's arms the enfolding skies,
With changeful benisons of sun and shower,
And moonlit silences on peaks austere.

Do battle with the Ocean's crested towers
When the wild gale upbuilds them to the sky
And the white foam-flags from their bastions fly
Or race the tempest through the cloudy plain
When the leashed lightnings from their bondage start,
And know thine ecstasy, outthrobbing pain,
Is but the breath of the eternal heart
Whose voice was Shelley's once and now is ours—"

[1889–93] (2019)

Algernon Charles Swinburne's poetry was considered controversial for its sexual themes, but it isn't clear whether that is the reason for Wharton's critique of him here. What is that "intense silence" and "deep calm" that she misses in his poetry? It is worth comparing Swinburne's poem about Shelley, also called "Cor Cordium," with Wharton's tribute.

🐚 Swinburne

WHY hast thou not the gift of reticence,
All other gifts possessing? Thou that wert
Born to become the Ocean's vocal heart
And echo of the thundering heavens immense,
Have not thy vigils taught thee that intense
Silence that seals the tempest? Let thine art
Learn the deep calm that sea and air impart
When tranquilly the baffled winds go hence.

Thin streams full-throated brawl along their beds,
Bruised by the shore's inhospitality
And railing at each rock that barricades
Their ineffectual struggle to be free,
But, from the welling of their fountain-heads,
Great rivers feel their kinship with the sea.

[1889–93] (2019)

As we have seen, Wharton often experimented with poetic forms. On the flyleaf of her 1916 copy of Paul-Louis Couchoud's *Sages et poètes d'Asie*, she practiced a few poems after the imagist model, derived from Asian poets, that was then popular with the contemporary poets Amy Lowell, Ezra Pound, Hilda Doolittle, and others. Later she published them, with slight changes in the wording, in the *Yale Review*. Wharton had recently been given an honorary doctorate by Yale University; her last visit to America was to receive the award. While we have no direct evidence that Wharton read Amy Lowell's poetry, she certainly knew of her: Lowell's older brother, Percy, had been best man at the Wharton wedding.

🐛 Lyrical Epigrams

I

MY little old dog:
A heart beat
At my feet.

II
Spring

A winter wind,
Primroses,
And the new furrow.

III
Friendship

The silence of midnight,
A dying fire,
And the best unsaid. . . .

IV

A pointed steeple
Above square trees—
Rustic France.

V

A blunt steeple
Over round trees—
Rural England.

VI
Soluntum

Across these giant ruins
The greatest cloud-shadows
Dart like little lizards.

[1916–20] (1920)

Wharton spent her life striving for beauty: in decor, in dress, in landscape, and in art. Here is a darker look at what such a devotion can mean for the devotee, be she artist or onlooker. Or perhaps it's a commentary on changing taste?

Beauty

AH, what is this new pang that makes us thine,
Beauty, thou goddess veiled from eyes of men,
Poised on blue pinnacles beyond our ken,
Or smothered in some incense-clouded shrine
Where all night long the blackening tapers shine?
Who put within thy hand the blade of pain
That streaks thy votaries with a bloody stain,
Who hid thy face, yet made it so divine?

Of old thy dwelling was in bodies fair,
Close-columned temples, gardens brimmed with bloom,
Now, grown intangible to search and prayer,
Thou hoverest like a phantom in the gloom,
And none can say that thou art here or there,
Bright as the daystar, darkling as our doom!

[1889–93] (2019)

These remaining poems are about works of art, all but the first written in the 1890s. "Raffaelle to the Fornarina" imagines the interplay between the Italian Renaissance painter Raphael (1483–1520) and his lover Margherita Luti, called "La Fornarina" because her father was a baker. Luti posed for numerous paintings, possibly as many as a half dozen of Raphael's paintings of the Madonna and child. Here Wharton is probably describing the *Madonna di San Sisto*, which hung in Dresden and was admired by Goethe, Nietzsche, and Wagner, and which she would have seen in her travels in Germany. Interesting that the sheltered sixteen-year-old had this knowledge of the painter's lover, and even more interesting that her parents included the poem in *Verses*.

Raffaelle to the Fornarina
(Sitting to him for a Madonna.)

KNOT up the filmy strands of golden hair
That veil your breast, yet leave its beauties bare;
In decent ripples backward let it flow,
Smooth-parted sideways from your placid brow.
Unclasp the clinging necklace from your throat,
And let this misty veil about you float,
As round the seraphs of my visions swim
Faint, roseate clouds to make their radiance dim
And bearable to dazzled human eyes,
Uplifted in a rapture of surprise.
Lay off your armlets now, and cover up
With dark blue folds that shoulder's dimpled slope;
Let naught appear to woo the grosser sense,
But ruling calm, and sacred innocence;

Subdue the pointed twinkle of your eye
Into a level, large serenity,
(Now comes the test) and let your mouth awhile
Be pressed into a faint, ascetic smile,
A pure reflection of the inward thought,
A chastened glow from fires celestial caught.

[1878] (1878)

The Tomb of Ilaria Guinigi, in Lucca, sculpted by Jacopo della Quercia
and much admired by John Ruskin.

Ilaria del Carretto Guinigi (1379–1405) (Wharton misspells her name) was a young Italian noblewoman who died in childbirth. Her tomb, sculpted by Jacopo della Quercia (c. 1374–1438), rests in the Cathedral of San Martino in Lucca and is considered one of the earliest masterpieces of the Renaissance. Wharton dated this poem 1889, the period when she was most interested in things Italian.

🦜 The Tomb of Ilaria Giunigi

ILARIA, thou that wert so fair and dear
That death would fain disown thee, grief made wise
With prophecy thy husband's widowed eyes,
And bade him call the master's art to rear
Thy perfect image on the sculptured bier,
With dreaming lids, hands laid in peaceful guise
Beneath the breast that seems to fall and rise,
And lips that at love's call should answer "Here!"

First-born of the Renascence, when thy soul
Cast the sweet robing of the flesh aside,
Into these lovelier marble limbs it stole,
Regenerate in art's sunrise clear and wide,
As saints who, having kept faith's raiment whole,
Change it above for garments glorified.

[1889] (1891)

Wharton sent this sonnet to Morton Fullerton, and he saved it with other poems she wrote for him. But she hadn't written it for Fullerton initially: the poem first appears in her archives, dated Venice 1895, considerably before they met. A notable change comes in line 10, which originally read, "(The piteous image Hope has wrought of you!)." If the "I" of the poem is Wharton herself, we cannot know who the "you" of the first version might have been. Lazzaro Sebastiani (c. 1425?–1512, also called Bastiani) was known for his technique of painting murals on very large canvas instead of on walls; in this case the lunette hangs above a doorway.

ᨀᨀ A Picture by Sebastiani
(in the Cathedral of Murano)

To the calm Virgin on her marble seat
The haggard saint two little angels brings,
Two little angels with new downy wings,
Clasped hands and innocently-moving feet,
Whom the calm Virgin gently bends to greet,
Despising not the day of little things—
While the wan saint, to whom earth's darkness clings,
Seems, through their lips, her mercy to entreat.

So to your thronèd presence in my heart,
(The tender image love has wrought of you),
Worn, baffled, doubting, to implore your grace
I bring the thoughts I think of you apart—
The thoughts that ever more their youth renew,
Because perpetually they see your face.

[1895] (2019)

Wharton here describes the backgrounds of two paintings that hang in the Louvre, the first by Jan van Eyck (1390–1441), and the second, of course, by Leonardo da Vinci (1452–1519). *La Vierge au Donateur* shows in the foreground the church donor Rolin being blessed by the baby Jesus and in close communion with the Virgin, who is dressed in a rich red robe and being crowned by an angel. The background of the painting is as Wharton describes it: bucolic and peaceful with a river flowing through the center. The two sides of the river are distinct. Behind the donor is a secular city with a church, houses, places of business, and vineyards and farmland beyond, whereas behind the Virgin is the celestial city. The river divides them, but a bridge unites them; the iconography points to Jesus as the savior who unites the earthly world with the heavenly one. It is interesting that Wharton chooses a classical allusion to Cybele, the Greek and Roman mother goddess, rather than to the Virgin to describe the fruitful and peaceful scene. The background of the *Mona Lisa* is famously mysterious, with dark mountains and tortuous pathways.

Wharton was to continue this interest in the backgrounds of paintings and places in her 1905 essay "Italian Backgrounds," published in her volume of the same name. In these backgrounds, the artist is "free to express his personality" and the viewer can "catch a glimpse of the life amid which the painting originated" (174).

🎵 Two Backgrounds

I

La Vierge au Donateur

Here by the ample river's argent sweep,
Bosomed in tilth and vintage to her walls,

Jan van Eyck, *La Vierge au Donateur*, one of Wharton's favorite paintings and the happier of her "Two Backgrounds."

Leonardo da Vinci, *Mona Lisa*, the darker of Wharton's "Two Backgrounds."

A tower-crowned Cybele in armoured sleep
The city lies, fat plenty in her halls,
With calm parochial spires that hold in fee
The friendly gables clustered at their base,
And, equipoised o'er tower and market-place,
The Gothic minster's winged immensity;
And in that narrow burgh, with equal mood,
Two placid hearts, to all life's good resigned,
Might, from the altar to the lych-gate, find
Long years of peace and dreamless plenitude.

II

Mona Lisa

Yon strange blue city crowns a scarpèd steep
No mortal foot hath bloodlessly essayed;
Dreams and illusions beacon from its keep,
But at the gate an Angel bares his blade;
And tales are told of those who thought to gain
At dawn its ramparts; but when evening fell
Far off they saw each fading pinnacle
Lit with wild lightnings from the heaven of pain;
Yet there two souls, whom life's perversities
Had mocked with want in plenty, tears in mirth,
Might meet in dreams, ungarmented of earth,
And drain Joy's awful chalice to the lees.

[?] (1892)

Many consider France's Gothic Chartres Cathedral, which dominates the landscape and can be seen from miles away, one of the world's greatest achievements in church architecture. Extraordinary for its exterior sculpture and its more than 150 richly colored medieval windows, it houses a relic of Mary's tunic and therefore has been the site of pilgrimage for eight hundred years. There are three enormous rose windows: North, South, and West, but not, despite how the poem ends, an East window. Wharton wrote about the cathedral later on in prose, twice. In *A Motor Flight Through France* she celebrated it, speaking of the "mystical heart of the apse" (78). Her fullest and most appreciative description came in *Fighting France*, in which she contrasted the splendor of the cathedral, which she visited just days before World War I began, with the scene in Paris as the city mobilized for war.

🐚 Chartres

I

Immense, august, like some Titanic bloom,
    The mighty choir unfolds its lithic core,
Petalled with panes of azure, gules and or,
    Splendidly lambent in the Gothic gloom,
And stamened with keen flamelets that illume
    The pale high-altar. On the prayer-worn floor,
By worshippers innumerous thronged of yore,
    A few brown crones, familiars of the tomb,
The stranded driftwood of Faith's ebbing sea—
    For these alone the finials fret the skies,
The topmost bosses shake their blossoms free,

While from the triple portals, with grave eyes,
Tranquil, and fixed upon eternity,
    The cloud of witnesses still testifies.

II

The crimson panes like blood-drops stigmatise
    The western floor. The aisles are mute and cold.
A rigid fetich in her robe of gold,
    The Virgin of the Pillar, with blank eyes,
Enthroned beneath her votive canopies,
    Gathers a meagre remnant to her fold.
The rest is solitude; the church, grown old,
    Stands stark and grey beneath the burning skies.
Well-nigh again its mighty framework grows
    To be a part of nature's self, withdrawn
From hot humanity's impatient woes;
    The floor is ridged like some rude mountain lawn,
And in the east one giant window shows
    The roseate coldness of an Alp at dawn.

[?] (1893)

A statue of Venus, now at the Louvre, was found in 1820 on the island of
Melos, thus giving it the name the Venus of Milo. Wharton here contem-
plates the mystery and history of the iconic statue, and with it the nature
of victory and beauty.

🏺 The So-called Venus of Milo

Who gave thee wings, thou wingless Victory,
That shouldst have shone o'er Athens to this hour?
Methinks the god of mutability,
Sole moon of destiny's rebellious sea,
Who lords it lonely o'er the tides of power,
One night when Athens in thy shelter slept
Saw thee on thy white citadel, and wept
To think thy splendour and thy strength should be
Like foam across the flood of ages swept.

Yea, he who feasts upon the fall of Kings,
Who thrones at Actium, as at Salamis,
Bound to thy throbbing shoulders his fleet wings,
And bade thee flee the storm's first thunderings,
Lest, losing thee, the after-world should miss
Its holiest heritage. Thy limbs august,
Beneath the senseless turf of Milo thrust,
Slept through the changes of a thousand Springs,
Then leapt again victorious from the dust.

But, born to this late century, that perceives
How often victory and defeat are one,

And how of both the baser part survives,
Thy guardian-god, in lieu of laurel-leaves
That fade and fall so soon beneath the sun,
Gave thee the name that, since the world began,
Outblossoms death, and bade thee be to man
The principle of beauty that outlives
Themistocles and Caesar, Christ and Pan.

[1889–93?] (2019)

Pisanello, *Portrait of a Princess* (Princess of Este).
The painting was acquired by the Louvre in 1893.

This touching painting by Pisanello (c. 1395–1455) holds a mystery: Which princess does it depict? Was it a happy one, painted on the occasion of her marriage? Or was it the one who would shortly be poisoned by her husband so that he could make a more advantageous marriage?

A Princess of the House of Este
(A Portrait by Pisanello in the Louvre.)

HER small pale face, with smoothly shaven brow
Rimmed by a battlement of yellow hair,
Like some strange flower, too fragile and too rare,
Stands slenderly against the blue's deep glow,
Laced with dark leaves and starred with buds ablow,
As in some garden where the saints repair,
Whose tranquil shade and bright inviolate air
No hurricanes of human longing know.

Yet on her cloak, in gold and jewels blent,
The passionate symbol of unrest behold,
A plant whose swift-expanding roots have rent
The vase that holds it. Was it thus you told
Your heart's desire, your century's discontent,
Sphinx with the childlike eyes untimely old?

[1893?] (2019)

Once again we see Wharton's imaginative use of Dante. Here she is thinking of *The Divine Comedy* as she contemplates Dante Gabriel Rossetti's sumptuous painting of Beata Beatrix, which she saw, perhaps for the first time, at an exhibition in New York in January 1893.

₩ The "Beata Beatrix" of Rossetti
"Guarda mi ben—ben son, ben son, Beatrice." *Purg*. XXX

THIS is that Beatrix whom the later seer,
Wandering with Dante through the woodland grim,
Met suddenly upon the streamlet's brim,
In the starred meadows of the upper sphere;
No symbolled creed, no Tuscan vision here,
But one whose eyes have seen (now grown more dim)
Faiths fall and Empires vanish like a dream,
Knowing the rose renews herself each year.

And when his gaze, that thought to meet the sun,
Had pierced the olive-cinctured veil she wore,
Methinks she smiled upon his travail done,
Whispering, "What matter though the way was sore?
Look on me, Poet, till our souls be one,
For I am Beauty, thou my servitor."

[1893?] (2019)

Arezzo is a city in southeast Tuscany noted for goldsmithing. Wharton is rarely wrong in her study of art and artifacts, but here she may be. Greek pottery is generally painted, whereas local Arretine red ware, derived from Roman tradition, is made in relief, thus molded. Wharton tries to capture in words of equivalent beauty the feel and look of an object she admires.

🏺 Mould and Vase
GREEK POTTERY OF AREZZO

HERE in the jealous hollow of the mould,
Faint, light-eluding, as templed in the breast
Of some rose-vaulted lotus, see the best
The artist had—the vision that unrolled
Its flying sequence till completion's hold
Caught the wild round and bade the dancers rest—
The mortal lip on the immortal pressed
One instant, ere the blindness and the cold.

And there the vase: immobile, exiled, tame,
The captives of fulfillment link their round,
Foot-heavy on the inelastic ground,
How different, yet how enviously the same!
Dishonoring the kinship that they claim,
As here the written word the inner sound.

[?] (1901)

Pietro Perugino, *Apollo and Marsyas*. Nothing about the painting—except perhaps the diving birds—suggests the impending violence.

In Greek mythology, Marsyas bragged of his flute playing, claiming it was more beautiful than any music Apollo could produce on his lyre. The god challenged him to a contest wherein the winner could do as he wished to the loser. Of course Apollo won; he pinned Marsyas to a tree and flayed him to death. Pietro Perugino (c. 1446–1523), the Italian Renaissance painter, captures the scene of an overconfident Marsyas just before the contest begins.

The "Apollo and Marsyas" of Perugino
(In the Louvre)

INSCRUTABLY serene the young god stands
In prescience inaccessible, his eyes
Bright with the fumes of mortal sacrifice,
The unfaltering lyre impatient for his hands.
Far valley-ward the windless pasture-lands
Whose sheltered paths his worshippers despise
Slope to the small walled city where the wise
Move tranquilly within fulfilled demands;

But on the hill-top, challenging the god,
Sits Marsyas, fluting his undaunted tune—
And smiling the god waits, foreseeing soon
The ultimate hour of him whose feet have trod
That perilous eminence, his bloody swoon,
His end unsorrowed and untended sod.

[?] (2019)

Looking at a bowl carved from jade, the speaker contemplates her soul. For the Chinese, jade symbolizes the Confucian virtues of benevolence, righteousness, wisdom, courage, and modesty, but Wharton's vision seems more Western and personal.

🜨 Jade

THE patient craftsman of the East who made
His undulant dragons of the veinèd jade,
And wound their sinuous volutes round the whole
Pellucid green redundance of the bowl,
Chiseled his subtle traceries with the same
Keen stone he wrought them in.
                    Nor praise, nor blame,
Nor gifts the years relinquish or refuse,
But only a grief commensurate with thy soul,
Shall carve it in a shape for gods to use.

[?] (1895)

Supernatural Thoughts

Wharton shared with her friend Henry James a love of ghost tales, and she wrote quite a number of them. Here we find poems, written throughout her lifetime, from the world of the dead and poems about thoughts that haunt one in the dead of night. They're chilling and fun to read, yet there is more to be found here. These poems explore the mystery of suffering and death, and they dip into the deep well of human fear: fear of dying and burial, fear of being forgotten and replaced, fear that this life is all there is, and fear that it is not all there is, that our spirits may continue to yearn and suffer through eternity.

One of Wharton's earliest short stories, "The Fullness of Life," is renowned for its depiction of a woman's nature as a "great house full of rooms," "and in the innermost room, the holy of holies, the soul sits alone and waits for a footstep that never comes" (14). The character who expresses such desolation, when she dies, is offered the chance to spend eternity in the company of her perfect soul mate, an opportunity she ultimately declines. "Gifts," a succinct sonnet written at about the same time, treats the same subject—using some of the same images—of a lonely soul who fails to meet her mate in life and hopes for another chance in death.

Gifts

WHEN we, who walk in paths unneighbourly,
Beyond the gateway of the grave shall meet
I shall make answer, as you pause and greet,
"Of all life's gifts what gifts have you for me?
Like masks across a crowded ballroom, we
Stumbled through life with unfamiliar feet,
And passed each other as strangers in the street,
Yet all the while you held my soul in fee!—

Behold my gifts; the sunset none but I
Remembered, or the book none other read;
The picture that I treasured for your eye;
And, last of all, these bitterest tears unshed—
Take them! but, if you bring no gift, go by,
And leave me doubly dead among the dead."

[1889–93] (2005)

Originally titled "The Ghost Wife," this poem makes an interesting comparison with the one that follows it, a more mature version written some thirty years later. What chills the reader is not only fearing death but also knowing that one doesn't have to die to be replaced in a husband's affections by a second wife.

The Dead Wife

MIGHT I, standing in the door
I shall open now no more,
Look into the room I knew
(That is known tonight to you)—

See if chair and table still
Keep their place—if flowers fill
That one opal cup he has
At his elbow—Venice glass—

If his inkstand freshly brims,
If no cloud his lamplight dims,
No rude hand has touched the heaps
On heaps of papers that he keeps—

Ah, once only if I might
Look upon it all tonight,
Then, strange wife, I'd turn away,
Content to let you have your day—

[1889–93] (2019)

In the Christian tradition, November 2 is All Souls' Day, set aside for honoring the dead. Catholics believe that through the prayer of the faithful on earth, the dead can be cleansed of their sins and allowed into heaven. All Saints' Day, November 1, is dedicated to the saints of the Church, to those who have obtained heaven. The following poems, however, rather than religious or sentimental, participate in that Gothic tradition of the thin layer between the realms of the living and the dead. Wharton is a much more accomplished poet by 1926; one can feel the influence of Walt Whitman in her images and cadences.

The First Year
[ALL SOULS' DAY]

I

HERE in my darkness
I lie in the depths of things,
As in a black wood whereof flowers and boughs are the roots,
And the moist-branching tendrils and ligaments,
Woven or spiralled or spreading, the roof of my head,
Blossomless, birdless, starless, skied with black earth,
A ponderous heaven.

But they forget,
Too often forget, and too soon, who above us
Brush the dead leaves from our mounds,
Scrape the moss from our names,
And feel safe,
They forget that one day in the year our earth becomes ether,

And the roots binding us loosen
As Peter's chains dropped for the Angel,
In that old story they read there;
Forget—do they seek to remember?—
That one day in the year we are with them,
Rejoin them, hear them, behold them, and walk the old ways
      with them—
One!

Tomorrow . . .
And already I feel
The harsh arms of ivy-coils loosening
Like a dead man's embrace,
I feel the cool worms from my hair
Rain like dew,
And the soft-muzzled moles boring deeper,
Down after the old dead that stir not,
Or just grumble: "Don't wake me," and turn
The nether side of their skulls to their head-slab . . .
While I . . . I their one-year neighbour,
Thrusting up like a willow in spring,
From my hair
Untwine the thick grass-hair carefully,
Unbind the cool roots from my lids,
Straining up, straining up with thin hands,
Scattering the earth like a cloud,
And stopping my ears from the cry,
Lower down,
Persistent, like a sick child's wail,

The cry of the girl just below me:
"Don't go, don't go . . ." the poor coward!

II

How light the air is!
I'm dizzy . . . my feet fly up . . .
And this mad confusion of things topsy-turvey,
With the friendly comprehensible roots all hidden,
In this queer world where one can't see how things happen,
But only what they become . . .
Was it always so queer and inexplicable?
Yes, but the fresh smell of things . . .
Are these apples in the wet grass, I wonder?
Sweet, sweet, sweet, the smell of the living!
And the far-off sky, and the stars,
And the quiet spaces between,
So that one can float and fly . . .
Why used we only to walk?

This is the gate—and the latch still unmended!
Yet how often I told him. . . . Ah, the scent of my box-border!
And a late clove-pink still unfrozen.
It's what they call a "mild November" . . .
I knew that, below there, by the way the roots kept pushing,
But I'd forgotten how tender it was on the earth . . .
So quickly the dead forget!
And the living? I think, after all, they remember,
With everything about them so unchanged,

And no leaden loam on their eyes.
Yes, surely, I know *he* remembers;
Whenever he touches the broken latch,
He thinks: "How often she asked me,
And how careless I was not to mend it!"
And smiles and sighs; then recalls
How we planted the box-border together,
Knee to knee in the wet, one November . . .
And the clove-pinks—
Here is the window.
They've put the green lamp on the table,
Where his books lie, heaped as of old—
Ah, thank God for the old disorder!
How I used to hate it, and now—
Now I could kiss the dust on the mirror, the pipe-ashes
Over everything—all the old mess
That no strange hand interferes with . . .
Bless him for that!

III

Just at first
This much contents me; why should I peer
Past the stripped arms of the rose, the metallic
Rattle of clematis dry as my hair,
There where June flushes and purples the window like sunset?
        I know
So well the room's other corner: the hearth
Where autumn logs smoulder,
The hob,

The kettle, the crane, the cushion he put for my feet,
And my Chair—
O Chair, always mine!
Do I dare?
What—the room so the same, his and mine,
Not a book changed, the inkstand uncleaned,
The old pipe-burn scarring the table,
The old rent in the rug, where I tripped
And he caught me—no woman's hand here
Has mended or marred; all's the same!
Why not dare, then? Oh, but to think,
If I stole to my chair, if I sat there,
Feet folded, arms stretched on the arms,
So quiet,
And waited for night and his coming . . .
Oh, think, when he came
And sank in the other chair, facing me,
Not a line of his face would alter,
Nor his hands fall like sun on my hair,
Nor the old dog jump on me, grinning
Yet cringing, because she half-knew
I'd found out the hole in my border,
And why my tallest auratum was dead—
But his face would be there, unseeing,
His eyes look through me;
And the old dog—not pausing
At her bowl for a long choking drink,
Or to bite the burrs from her toes, and stretch
Sideward to the fire, dreaming over their tramp in the stubble—
Would creep to his feet

Bristling a little . . .
And I,
I should be there, in the old place,
All the old life bubbling up in me,
And to him no more felt than the sap
Struggling up unseen in the clematis—
Ah, then, then, then I were dead!

But what *was* I then? Lips and hands only—
Since soul cannot reach him without them?
Oh, heavy grave of the flesh,
Did I never once reach to him through you?
I part the branches and look . . .

IV

O my Chair . . .
But who sits in you? One like me
Aflame yet invisible!
Only I, with eyes death-anointed,
Can see her young hair, and the happy heart riding
The dancing sea of her breast!
Then she too is waiting—
And young as I was?
Was she always there?
Were her lips between all our kisses?
Did her hands know the folds of his hair?
Did she hear what I said when I loved him?
Was the room never empty? Not once?
When I leaned in that chair, which one of us two did he see?

Did he feel us both on his bosom?
How strange! If I spoke to her now she would hear me,
She alone . . .
Would tell me all, through her weeping,
Or rise up and curse me, perhaps—
As I might her, were she living!
But since she is dead, I will go—
Go home, and leave them together . . .
I will go back to my dungeon,
Go back, and never return;
Lest another year, in my chair,
I find one sitting,
One whom he sees, and the old dog fears not, but springs on . . .
I will not suffer what *she* must have suffered, but creep
To my bed in the dark,
And mind how the girl below called to me,
Called up through the mound and the grave-slabs:
"Do not go! Do not go! Do not go!"

[?] (1926)

ALL SOVLS

By EDITH WHARTON

I

A THIN moon faints in the sky o'erhead,
And dumb in the churchyard lie the dead.
Walk we not, Sweet, by garden ways,
Where the late rose hangs and the phlox delays,
But forth of the gate and down the road,
Past the church and the yews, to their dim abode.
For it's turn of the year and All Souls' night,
When the dead can hear and the dead have sight.

II

Fear not that sound like wind in the trees:
It is only their call that comes on the breeze;
Fear not the shudder that seems to pass:
It is only the tread of their feet on the grass;
Fear not the drip of the bough as you stoop:
It is only the touch of their hands that grope—
For the year's on the turn, and it's All Souls' night,
When the dead can yearn and the dead can smite.

III

And where should a man bring his sweet to woo
But here, where such hundreds were lovers too?
Where lie the dead lips that thirst to kiss,
The empty hands that their fellows miss,
Where the maid and her lover, from sere to green,
Sleep bed by bed, with the worm between?
For it's turn of the year and All Souls' night,
When the dead can hear and the dead have sight.

"All Souls" as it appeared in *Scribner's Magazine* in 1909, decoration by Franklin Booth.

IV

And now that they rise and walk in the cold,
Let us warm their blood and give youth to the old.
Let them see us and hear us, and say: "Ah, thus
In the prime of the year it went with us!"
Till their lips drawn close, and so long unkist,
Forget they are mist that mingles with mist!
For the year's on the turn, and it's All Souls' night,
When the dead can burn and the dead can smite.

V

Till they say, as they hear us—poor dead, poor dead!—
"Just an hour of this, and our age-long bed—
Just a thrill of the old remembered pains
To kindle a flame in our frozen veins,
Just a touch, and a sight, and a floating apart,
As the chill of dawn strikes each phantom heart—
For it's turn of the year and All Souls' night,
When the dead can hear, and the dead have sight."

VI

And where should the living feel alive
But here in this wan white humming hive,
As the moon wastes down, and the dawn turns cold,
And one by one they creep back to the fold?
And where should a man hold his mate and say:
"One more, one more, ere we go their way"?
For the year's on the turn, and it's All Souls' night,
When the living can learn by the churchyard light.

VII

And how should we break faith who have seen
Those dead lips plight with the mist between,
And how forget, who have seen how soon
They lie thus chambered and cold to the moon?
How scorn, how hate, how strive, we too,
Who must do so soon as those others do?
For it's All Souls' night, and break of the day,
And behold, with the light the dead are away. . . .

All Souls

I

A THIN moon faints in the sky o'erhead,
And dumb in the churchyard lie the dead.
Walk we not, Sweet, by garden ways,
Where the late rose hangs and the phlox delays,
But forth of the gate and down the road,
Past the church and the yews, to their dim abode.
For it's turn of the year and All Souls' night,
When the dead can hear and the dead have sight.

II

Fear not that sound like wind in the trees:
It is only their call that comes on the breeze;
Fear not the shudder that seems to pass:
It is only the tread of their feet on the grass;
Fear not the drip of the bough as you stoop:
It is only the touch of their hands that grope—
For the year's on the turn, and it's All Souls' night,
When the dead can yearn and the dead can smite.

III

And where should a man bring his sweet to woo
But here, where such hundreds were lovers too?
Where lie the dead lips that thirst to kiss,

The empty hands that their fellows miss,
Where the maid and her lover, from sere to green,
Sleep bed by bed, with the worm between?
For it's turn of the year and All Souls' night,
When the dead can hear and the dead have sight.

IV

And now they rise and walk in the cold,
Let us warm their blood and give youth to the old.
Let them see us and hear us, and say: "Ah, thus
In the prime of the year it went with us!"
Till their lips drawn close, and so long unkist,
Forget they are mist that mingles with mist!
For the year's on the turn, and it's All Souls' night,
When the dead can burn and the dead can smite.

V

Till they say, as they hear us—poor dead, poor dead!—
"Just an hour of this, and our age-long bed—
Just a thrill of the old remembered pains
To kindle a flame in our frozen veins,
A touch, and a sight, and a floating apart,
As the chill of dawn strikes each phantom heart—
For it's turn of the year and All Souls' night,
When the dead can hear, and the dead have sight."

VI

And where should the living feel alive
But here in this wan white humming hive,
As the moon wastes down, and the dawn turns cold,
And one by one they creep back to the fold?
And where should a man hold his mate and say:
"One more, one more, ere we go their way"?
For the year's on the turn, and it's All Souls' night,
When the living can learn by the churchyard light.

VII

And how should we break faith who have seen
Those dead lips plight with the mist between,
And how forget, who have seen how soon
They lie thus chambered and cold to the moon?
How scorn, how hate, how strive, we too,
Who must do so soon as those others do?
For it's All Souls' night, and break of the day,
And behold, with the light the dead are away. . . .

[?] (1909)

🐚 All Saints

ALL so grave and shining see they come
    From the blissful ranks of the forgiven,
Though so distant wheels the nearest crystal dome,
    And the spheres are seven.

Are you in such haste to come to earth,
    Shining ones, the Wonder on your brow,
To the low poor places of your birth,
    And the day that must be darkness now?

Does the heart still crave the spot it yearned on
    In the grey and mortal years,
The pure flame the smoky hearth it burned on,
    The clear eye its tears?

Was there, in the narrow range of living,
    After all the wider scope?
In the old old rapture of forgiving,
    In the long long flight of hope?

Come you, from free sweep across the spaces,
    To the irksome bounds of mortal law,
From the all-embracing Vision, to some face's
    Look that never saw?

Never we, imprisoned here, had sought you,
    Lured you with the ancient bait of pain,
Down the silver current of the light-years brought you
    To the beaten round again—

Is it you, perchance, who ache to strain us
    Dumbly to the dim transfigured breast,
Or with tragic gesture would detain us
    From the age-long search for rest?

Is the labour then more glorious than the laurel,
    The learning than the conquered thought?
Is the meed of men the righteous quarrel,
    Not the justice wrought?

Long ago we guessed it, faithful ghosts,
    Proudly chose the present for our scene,
And sent out indomitable hosts
    Day by day to widen our demesne.

Sit you by our hearth-stone, lone immortals,
    Share again the bitter wine of life!
Well we know, beyond the peaceful portals
    There is nothing better than our strife,

Nought more thrilling than the cry that calls us,
    Spent and stumbling, to the conflict vain,
After each disaster that befalls us
    Nerves us for a sterner strain,

And, when flood or foeman shakes the sleeper
    In his moment's lapse from pain,
Bids us fold our tents, and flee our kin, and deeper
    Drive into the wilderness again.

[?] (1909)

Instead of ghosts coming back to the world, here we have a living person bound by the dead. "Antre swart" is a dark cavern.

A Grave

THOUGH life should come
With all its marshalled honours, trump and drum,
To proffer you the captaincy of some
Resounding exploit, that shall fill
Man's pulses with commemorative thrill,
And be a banner to far battle days
For truths unrisen upon untrod ways,
What would your answer be,
O heart once brave?
Seek otherwhere; for me,
I watch beside a grave.

Though to some shining festival of thought
The sages call you from steep citadel
Of bastioned argument, whose rampart gained
Yields the pure vision passionately sought,
In dreams known well,
But never yet in wakefulness attained,
How should you answer to their summons, save:
I watch beside a grave?

Though Beauty, from her fane within the soul
Of fire-tongued seers descending,
Or from the dream-lit temples of the past

With feet immortal wending,
Illuminate grief's antre swart and vast
With half-veiled face that promises the whole
To him who holds her fast,
What answer could you give?
Sight of one face I crave,
One only while I live;
Woo elsewhere; for I watch beside a grave.

Though love of the one heart that loves you best,
A storm-tossed messenger,
Should beat its wings for shelter in your breast,
Where clung its last year's nest,
The nest you built together and made fast
Lest envious winds should stir,
And winged each delicate thought to minister
With sweetness far-amassed
To the young dreams within—
What answer could it win?
The nest was whelmed in sorrow's rising wave,
Nor could I reach one drowning dream to save;
I watch beside a grave.

[?] (1909)

Wharton wrote this poem during the summer of 1908, when she was living in her beloved Massachusetts home, The Mount. Yet she chose not to include it in the volume that she was preparing that fall for Scribner's. One might ask why: Was it not good enough? Too revealing? Or perhaps it just didn't fit with the general scheme of the volume, *Artemis to Actæon*, in which the previous three poems appeared. We have all been troubled by thoughts that keep us awake; Poe, famously, embodied it as a raven.

🐚 A Knock

IT was not the blind's tap against the pane
  That broke my sleep,
But the knock of the same old thought against the brain.
  I heard it creep

Down the dim road, across the misty lawn,
  Under black boughs;
Each night it wakes me, sits with me till dawn,
  Then through the house

Steals masked and sated from the harmless light;
  But all the day
It lurks and watches, barely out of sight,
  Secret and gray.

The shadows hide it, and the silence hides,
  Till night again;
Then through the unsuspecting house it glides,
  Knocks at my brain,

Unlatches all the windows of the soul,
    Points out to me
From every one the lifeless wastes that roll
    To a dead sea,

And on the dead sea, under a dead sky,
    Moved by no gale,
Shows, crawling toward me like a crawling fly,
    The same black sail.

Each night I lie and wait for that low rap
    Against the brain,
That used to be no more than the blind's tap
    Upon the pane.

[1908] (2019)

Sometimes life itself is more frightening than death, as these next two poems reveal. Those who say Wharton was unaware of, or never wrote about, the underside of life will find evidence here to refute that judgment.

🪻 The Masque of Life

FAR fearfuller to late-born eyes
Than mediaeval masque of death,
The masque of them that draw their breath
From springs of madness, misery and vice.

In hideous line I see them move,
Each scarred with some ancestral stain,
Ere they beheld this world of pain
Outcasts from hope and righteousness and love,

And louder grows their crowding tread,
The lame, the leprous, and the blind,
The thrice corrupt, flesh, heart, and mind,
Born of old sins, long-buried but not dead.

Still hurrying on from hand to hand
Heredity's high torch they come;
Some totter to the grave, but some
As yet are little children in the land.

Onward, fell harbingers of strife,
They hasten at Time's chariot wheels,
Lust, famine, slaughter at their heels—
Where shall I hide me from the Masque of Life?

[1889–93] (2019)

Weltschmerz, world weariness, is more than a Romantic conceit for the speaker of this poem. As in "The Masque of Life," the speaker confronts the manifold horrors of life, but instead of being haunted by them wants to embrace them and protect the world just as Winkelried, hero of Swiss legend, threw himself in front of the spears of an invading army so that his fellow soldiers could advance and defend their country.

⚘ Weltschmerz

SOME awful hours there are, when the world's pain
Transfixes me, and suddenly I hear
The echo of all the brutal blows that rain
On animals and children, far and near;

When Hell's antiphony of oaths and lies
Thickens the air to foulness, and the groan
Of drowning sailors under leaden skies
Mingles its horror with the maniac's moan;

When with dilated eyes I seem to see,
Forth-marshalled by the mocking hand of Time,
A palsied, plague-struck, starving company,
Born of the old heredity of crime;

Then, from the sight of June's ambrosial blue,
From tipple of birds, and blossoms breaking free,
Like one whom Furies without pause pursue,
Into the outer night I long to flee,

And there, as eagerly as Mothers strain
To hungry hearts the child they love the best,
Gather, like Winkelried, the shafts of pain
Of all the world into my bleeding breast.

[1889–93] (2019)

And sometimes Death seems as real and strong as a god. In keeping with her admiration for Dante's *Divine Comedy*, Wharton here explores the realm of Death using Dante's rhymed, interlinked terza rima form.

🎵 Terza Rima

BRING to the temple of the throne of Death,
Wan worshippers, no tributary weight
Of blinding tears and pained, reluctant breath,

No lonely love that moans disconsolate,
Like a lost wind across a starless sky,
No starving hope or unrequited hate;

Not these the trophies that delight his eye
In the pale precincts of his awful reign;
He knows the tyrant's long satiety

Of sobs and blood and immemorial pain;
The cry of souls borne downward in the strife
Clamours against his iron gates in vain,

Anguish and madness in his courts are rife,
Old age lies hopeless at his icy throne,
While he sits dreaming of the joys of life

And all sweet treasures, soon to be his own.
Then bring, ye votaries, with rose-girt head
And balmy torch by Love's own breathing blown,

Bring to the ghastly concourse of the dead
All that is twined with life, as ivy clings,
To a green bough irrevocably wed;

Lips where Love's kisses fain would fold their wings,
Eyes, that the dawn still thrills to happy tears,
Hearts that o'erflow with joy's perennial springs,

Youth that not yet has paused to count its years.
These, these are Death's desire; he keeps for these
Guerdons of anguish, and dark draughts of fears,

With desperation lurking in the lees.
He loves to slake at laughter's bubbling well
The burning thirst that tears no more appease,

He loves to woo to his grey citadel
Light feet that loiter idly by the way,
And deck the columns of his inmost cell

With the young confidence that scorns decay,
As storm-winds ravish to their mountain-bed
The new-blown garlands of the radiant May.

Then bring, ye votaries, with rose-girt head
And balmy torch by Love's own breathing blown,
Bring, to propitiate your idol dread,
All that makes life most lovely, for his own.

[1889–93] (2019)

On Death and a Philosophy of Life

D eath appears frequently in Wharton's poetry. Sunsets occasion thoughts of death; characters in her dramatic monologues often speak from their deathbeds; many of her public poems were occasioned by death; and even in her love poems death appears as the finality against which love and heartbreak can be measured.

Balancing this awareness of death, we can find a corresponding philosophy of life developed over the course of her more than sixty years of writing poetry. At seventy, in thinking about her life and old age, Wharton offered these words:

> In spite of illness, in spite even of the arch-enemy sorrow, one *can* remain alive long past the usual date of disintegration if one is unafraid of change, insatiable in intellectual curiosity, interested in big things, and happy in small ways (*A Backward Glance* xix).

The following poems contemplate not only death, but also life, particularly the traits of mind and character we develop to comprehend and abide our emotions and experiences. Patience, opportunities, desire, hope, grief, duty, vengeance, old age: all are examined. Many are sonnets, that most elegant and controlled of verse forms, suggesting a desire to contain overwhelming feelings. While it's not possible to date all of Wharton's poems, most of these are organized roughly in chronological order, giving us a sense of her concerns at different stages of her life and the maturation of her philosophy.

We have this poem—a prayer, really—copied down in the hand of Emelyn Washburn, a childhood friend of Wharton's whose father was the minister of the church attended by the Jones family. Evidently young Edith wrote the poem to be read at an Easter service. As one would expect, religion offers consolation for heavy hearts.

Easter

WHEN life is heavy and the dross
Of earth about me clings
I only feel my leaden cross
Not mine immortal wings—
Then stoop into mine heart and roll
The stone of sin away,
And dawn, O Christ, upon my soul
A living Easter day!

So let me rise to thee from whom
So oft my footsteps fall!
What are to thee the guarded Tomb,
The silence and the pall?
Redeemer! As thy body broke
From all those bonds away
And the lone sepulchre forsook
On that first Easter day

So snap the chains of doubt and wrong
That cling about me here;
When e'er I falter, make me strong;

Where e'er I grope be near
To guide like a steadfast light,
Along the heavenly way
And snatch me up into one bright
Perpetual Easter day—

[1876] (2019)

This poem, written in the month Wharton turned fifteen, suggests a sophisticated understanding both of human nature and a developing, serious theology, which includes an awareness of death. She writes in rhymed couplets, a form popular in the eighteenth century for elevated subjects, though she has not yet mastered the heroic couplet with its caesura midline.

❧ Heaven

NOT over roof and spire doth Heaven lie,
Star-sentinelled from our humanity,
Beyond humble reach of every day.
And only near us when we weep or pray;
But rather in the household and the street,
Where loudest is the noise of hurrying feet,
Where hearts beat thickest, where our duties call,
Where watchers sit, where tears in silence fall.
We know not, or forget, there is no line
That marks our human off from our divine;
For all one household, all one family
In different chambers labouring are we;
God leaves the doors between them open wide,
Knowing how life and death are close allied,
And though across the threshold, in the gloom,
We cannot see into that other room,
It may be that the dear ones watching there
Can hear our cry of passionate despair,
And wait unseen to lead us through the door
When twilight comes, and all our work is o'er.

[January 1877] (1878)

Beginning at a young age, Wharton used the occasion of death to write poems of grief and consolation. This one, written when she was sixteen, eulogizes the child of a family friend, a deaf girl. The title comes from Luke 8:54, when Jesus raises the daughter of Jairus from the dead.

🦋 "Maiden, Arise"

SHE, whom through life her God forbade to hear
The voices of her nearest and most dear,
So that she dwelt, amid the hum and rush
Of cities, in a vast, eternal hush,
Yet heard the first low calling of the voice
That others had not heeded in the noise,
And rising, when it whispered "Come with me,"
Followed the form that others could not see,
Smiling, perchance, in death at last to hear
The voices of the Angels fill her ear,
While the great silent void that closed her round
Was overflowed with rippled floods of sound,
And the dumb past in Alleluias drowned.

[March 1877] (1878)

The following poems reveal a young woman formulating some precepts to live by. Presented in the context of religious thought, this poem suggests at least a hope that some opportunities will come to this carefully chaperoned young lady.

The "two that trode the Eastern street" refers to the two apostles who were accompanied by Jesus to Emmaus but did not recognize him even as they spoke with him (Luke 24:13-35).

🐝 Opportunities

WHO knows his opportunities? They come
Not trumpet-tongued from Heaven, but small and dumb,
Not beckoning from the future's promised land,
But in the narrow present close at hand.
They walk beside us with unsounding feet,
And like those two that trode the Eastern street
And with their Saviour bartered thought for thought,
Our eyes are holden and we know them not.

[1878] (1878)

The next two poems are some of Wharton's earliest published in peri-
odicals. They seem to reflect the young writer's search for the proper
deportment and temper of a woman, particularly in the face of desire,
disappointment, and constraint.

🐛 Wants

WE women want so many things;
    And first we call for happiness, —
The careless boon the hour brings,
    The smile, the song, and the caress.

And when the fancy fades, we cry,
    Nay, give us one on whom to spend
Our heart's desire! When Love goes by
    With folded wings, we seek a friend.

And then our children come, to prove
    Our hearts but slumbered, and can wake;
And when they go, we're fain to love
    Some other woman's for their sake.

But when both love and friendship fail,
    We cry for duty, work to do;
Some end to gain beyond the pale
    Of self, some height to journey to.

And then, before our task is done,
    With sudden weariness oppressed,

We leave the shining goal unwon,
    And only ask for rest.

[1880?] (1880)

🪶 Patience

PATIENCE and I have traveled hand in hand
    So many days that I have grown to trace
    The lines of sad, sweet beauty in her face,
And all its veilèd depths to understand.

Not beautiful is she to eyes profane;
    Silent and unrevealed her holy charms;
    But, like a mother's, her serene, strong arms
Uphold my footsteps on the path of pain.

I long to cry,—her soft voice whispers, "Nay!"
    I seek to fly, but she restrains my feet;
    In wisdom stern, yet in compassion sweet,
She guides my helpless wanderings, day by day.

O my Beloved, life's golden visions fade,
    And one by one life's phantom joys depart;
    They leave a sudden darkness in the heart,
And patience fills their empty place instead.

[1880] (1880)

Wharton revisited the subject of patience when she was in her early thirties in this previously unpublished sonnet. Instead of writing in the first person, she creates a character who exemplifies that difficult virtue.

🦋 A Patient Soul

CLOSE to the rainbow joys of life she stands,
As beggars at a jeweller's window lean
Against the brittle panes that intervene
Between the diamonds and their hungry hands,
And yet, although her quiet gaze commands
Full view of those who gayly enter in
And choose among the treasures what had been
The banquet of her life, her soul expands
With gladness, and she thinks, "My joy shall be
Fit crownal for that fairer head—shall shine
Brighter on that light bosom than for me
And, being hers, shall thus be doubly mine."

Christ, hast thou not, for one so like to thee,
After life's fast some festival divine?

[1889–93] (2019)

Like the previous poem, this sonnet appears in the poetry notebook Wharton kept when she was in her early thirties. No longer a child, she contemplates an opportunity not lost, but deliberately renounced. Death appears as a measuring stick against which to evaluate the quality of one's life and here, as in the next few poems, the resulting sorrow must be somehow absorbed and assimilated.

🎵 Renunciation

WHAT if when death shall come you cry out, "Wait!
Not mine the breath you thirst for, O not mine,
For I have missed the hour supreme, divine,
That for life's emptiness shall compensate,
That yet must come, although it come so late,
Once let me drink its draught of maddening wine,
Through all my midnight let its sunrise shine,
Then take me ere my blessedness abate!"

And what if death shall answer, "Many a day
Ere this, that hour lay pleading at your feet.
Have you forgotten how you turned away
From the sweet joy you had gone forth to meet?"—
Ah then, my soul, be strong in death to say,
"The grief I chose instead was far more sweet."

[1889–93] (2019)

First published in 1898, then included in *Artemis to Actæon*, "The One Grief" could be read as a poem of growing up, of learning to understand the darker places of human life concealed from a sheltered, happy child. The first-person narration makes it more intimate than the poem that follows, which was also in *Artemis to Actæon*.

🎐 The One Grief

ONE grief there is, the helpmeet of my heart,
    That shall not from me till my days be sped,
    That walks beside me in sunshine and in shade,
And hath in all my fortunes equal part.
At first I feared it, and would often start
    Aghast to find it bending o'er my bed,
    Till usage slowly dulled the edge of dread,
And one cold night I cried: *How warm thou art!*

Since then we two have travelled hand in hand,
    And, lo, my grief has been interpreter
For me in many a fierce and alien land
Whose speech young Joy had failed to understand,
    Plucking me tribute of red gold and myrrh
From desolate whirlings of the desert sand.

[?] (1898)

🐝 Grief

I

On immemorial altitudes august
Grief holds her high dominion. Bold the feet
That climb unblenching to that stern retreat
Whence, looking down, man knows himself but dust.
There lie the mightiest passions, earthward thrust
Beneath her regnant footstool, and there meet
Pale ghosts of buried longings that were sweet,
With many an abdicated "shall" and "must."

For there she rules omnipotent, whose will
Compels a mute acceptance of her chart;
Who holds the world, and lo! it cannot fill
Her mighty hand; who will be served apart
With uncommunicable rites, and still
Surrender of the undivided heart.

II

She holds the world within her mighty hand,
And lo! it is a toy for babes to toss,
And all its shining imagery but dross,
To those that in her awful presence stand;
As sun-confronting eagles o'er the land

That lies below, they send their gaze across
The common intervals of gain and loss,
And hope's infinitude without a strand.

But he who, on that lonely eminence,
Watches too long the whirling of the spheres
Through dim eternities, descending thence
The voices of his kind no longer hears,
And, blinded by the spectacle immense,
Journeys alone through all the after years.

[?] (1909)

Does the line "Affronts at last its final boundary" indicate that this is a poem about death? Or is it about overwhelming grief? Does the poem belong with other love and heartbreak poems? Or is it another landscape of the imagination? It can also be read as seeking a map for the soul to navigate life's inevitable sorrows.

🌿 Sorrow's Sea—

LEAGUE, leaguc on league, the unsubsiding sea
Stretches its tumult to the sky's fixed rim,
And where the utmost Eastern star grows dim
Affronts at last its final boundary;
Even hence the spirit's winged alacrity
Accepts that shore; but, lo, the waves that brim
Innumerously the nearer gaze; to him
Who scans the flood how shall they numbered be?

Even so, at last, Oblivion's shores abide
The onset of Grief's ocean, O my soul,
For Time hath spanned its unimagined tide
And framed a chart to guide thee to thy goal;
But who that stands upon the hither side
Shall count the waves of sorrow as they roll?

[?] (2019)

For the despairing speaker of this poem, in the absence of God, Duty becomes not a taskmistress but a refuge.

🐚 The New Litany

DUTY, O Mother of stricken souls that flee
From pleasure's haggard portals, hold me fast
Until this agony be overpast—
Whom have I, Mother, in heaven or earth but thee?

Of old, O Mother, a Virgin pure as thou,
But tenderer-bosomed, at the throne of God
Pleaded for men—but now a darkling cloud
Conceals God's footstool, and her bended brow.

Viceregent of the past, O latest-born
Of the last race of gods, and most austere,
The seal of whose disciples is a tear,
Their livery is the crowd's unreasoning scorn,

Lean from the throne God leaves untenanted
And summon me to that high solitude,
Once with the wings of Angels rainbow-hued,
And populous with many a haloed head!

O thou the new Persephone, enthroned
Above the ghostly herd of them that died
For creeds discredited and hopes belied,
Wilt thou too fall and leave the heavens unowned?

Nay, goddess of the living as the dead,
Man's utmost refuge from the grief that smites,
And from the scorpion-sting of dead delights,
Leave not thy worshippers uncomforted!

Renew thy primal majesty, uphold
Our wavering footsteps, and proclaim to all
That, though whole dynasties of gods may fall,
Yet righteousness is sacred as of old.

[1889–93] (2019)

This poem offers another life philosophy. That it was placed very close in her notebook to "The New Litany" and "Weltschmerz" suggests that perhaps Wharton was struggling with existential questions when she reached her thirties.

Not what we win but what we lose
Is the best heritage of years—
The baser joys our hearts refuse,
The cross, the abstinence, the tears—

Unsquandered are the purest powers,
The dearest lips are still unkissed,
And crowned with sacramental hours
Is the one joy we sought and missed—

[1889–93] (2019)

The Roman senator Caecina Paetus was condemned to death in 42 CE for his involvement in a conspiracy against Emperor Claudius. To give him courage, his wife, Arria, first stabbed herself, then passed the dagger to Paetus, saying, "Paete, non dolet!" ("It does not hurt, Paetus!").

🦋 Non Dolet!

AGE after age the fruit of knowledge falls
To ashes on men's lips;
Love fails, faith sickens, like a dying tree
Life sheds its dreams that no new spring recalls;
The longed-for ships
Come empty home or founder on the deep,
And eyes first lose their tears and then their sleep.

So weary a world it lies, forlorn of day,
And yet not wholly dark,
Since evermore some soul that missed the mark
Calls back to those agrope
In the mad maze of hope,
"Courage, my brothers—I have found the way!"

The day is lost? What then?
What though the straggling rear-guard of the fight
Be whelmed in fear and night,
And the flying scouts proclaim
That death has gripped the van—
Ever the heart of man
Cheers on the hearts of men!

"It hurts not!" dying cried the Roman wife;
And one by one
The leaders in the strife
Fall on the blade of failure and exclaim:
"The day is won!"

[?] (1909)

As with the last poem, this can be read as a poem of either hope or despair.
Why the title "A Hunting-Song"?

🐗 A Hunting-Song

Hunters, where does Hope nest?
Not in the half-oped breast,
Nor the young rose,
Nor April sunrise—those
With a quick wing she brushes,
The wide world through,
Greets with the throat of thrushes,
Fades from as fast as dew.

But, would you spy her sleeping,
Cradled warm,
Look in the breast of weeping,
The tree stript by storm;
But, would you bind her fast,
Yours at last,
Bed-mate and lover,
Gain the last headland bare
That the cold tides cover,
There may you capture her, there,
Where the sea gives to the ground
Only the drift of the drowned.

Yet, if she slips you, once found,
Push to her uttermost lair
In the low house of despair.
There will she watch by your head,
Sing to you till you be dead,
Then, with your child in her breast,
In another heart build a new nest.

[1907?] (1909)

The Eumenides—also called the Furies—in Greek mythology were the female deities of vengeance. Eumenides is a euphemistic name for them—those who do good—meant to appease these terrible creatures. They are a recurring presence in Wharton's work, most notably when Lily Bart is haunted by them in *The House of Mirth*. The poem refers to Orestes as the victim who sought Apollo's grace. As earlier depicted in "The Oresteia," Orestes murdered his mother and thus sought relief from the vengeance of the Furies. This is Wharton's meditation on guilt and a heart at peace.

🐚 The Eumenides

THINK you we slept within the Delphic bower,
What time our victim sought Apollo's grace?
Nay, drawn into ourselves, in that deep place
Where good and evil meet, we bode our hour.
For not inexorable is our power,
And we are hunted of the prey we chase,
Soonest gain ground on them that flee apace,
And draw temerity from hearts that cower.

Shuddering we gather in the house of ruth,
And on the fearful turn a face of fear,
But they to whom the ways of doom are clear
Not vainly named us the Eumenides.
Our feet are faithful in the paths of truth,
And in the constant heart we house at peace.

[?] (1909)

In the time of Ancient Egypt, some five thousand years ago, Thuban was used as the pole star. Egyptians built the Great Pyramid of Cheops and other structures so that Thuban could be seen, by day and by night, from the bottom of the central passage. But because our solar system continues to move, Thuban is no longer visible and our pole star is now Polaris, commonly known as the North Star. A clepsydra is an ancient Greek timepiece that used the regulated flow of water to measure time.

Wharton, a great reader of science, here meditates on what changes in the universe and what endures. Of interest to the literary historian: this poem elicited a letter of praise from the Amherst College professor David Todd, remembered now because his wife, Mabel Loomis Todd, was the lover of Emily Dickinson's brother and the editor of the poems Dickinson left at her death.

⚜ The Old Pole Star

BEFORE the clepsydra had bound the days
Man tethered Change to his fixed star, and said:
"The elder races, that long since are dead,
Marched by that light; it swerves not from its base
Though all the worlds about it wax and fade."

When Egypt saw it, fast in reeling spheres,
Her Pyramids shaft-centred on its ray
She reared and said: "Long as this star holds sway
In uninvaded ether, shall the years
Revere my monuments—" and went her way.

The Pyramids abide; but through the shaft
That held the polar pivot, eye to eye,
Look now—blank nothingness! As though Change laughed
At man's presumption and his puny craft,
The star has slipped its leash and roams the sky.

Yet could the immemorial piles be swung
A skyey hair's-breadth from their rooted base,
Back to the central anchorage of space,
Ah, then again, as when the race was young,
Should they behold the beacon of the race!

Of old, men said: "The Truth is there: we rear
Our faith full-centred on it. It was known
Thus of the elders who foreran us here,
Mapped out its circuit in the shifting sphere,
And found it, 'mid mutation, fixed alone."

Change laughs again, again the sky is cold,
And down that fissure now no star-beam glides.
Yet they whose sweep of vision grows not old
Still at the central point of space behold
Another pole-star: for the Truth abides.

[1908] (1909)

Wharton wrote several poems called "Life." This one was published in *Scribner's Magazine* in 1894, when she was thirty-two and still in the process of sorting her years and days into order and beauty.

Life

LIFE, like a marble block, is given to all,
A blank, inchoate mass of years and days,
Whence one with ardent chisel swift essays
Some shape of strength or symmetry to call;
One shatters it in bits to mend a wall;
One in a craftier hand the chisel lays,
And one, to wake the mirth in Lesbia's gaze,
Carves it apace in toys fantastical.

But least is he who, with enchanted eyes
Filled with high visions of fair shapes to be,
Muses which god he shall immortalize
In the proud Parian's perpetuity,
Till twilight warns him from the punctual skies
That the night cometh wherein none shall see.

[1894?] (1894)

This sanguine poem appears late in Wharton's poetry notebook and suggests a contentment and gratitude for life.

🦋 Life

How sweet, O Life, to wake at dawn and find
Thy face beside the pillow,—ah, how sweet
To hear once more the day's familiar feet
Through lessening caverns of the darkness wind,
And know the friendly faces of my kind
Once more shall smile upon me in the street,
And the full flood of being freshly beat
Through the dry channels of my quickened mind.

How sweet, O World, to know that thou and I
Another day are lovers, ere we part;
Mine the blue promise of the rainless sky,
And mine the unfurling rose's fiery heart;
And when comes darkness and the last goodbye,
Mine the remembrance of how fair thou art!—

[1889–93] (2019)

Here we move into poems more specifically about death. Wharton was thirty-two when she published this double sonnet, which questions the value of experience in the face of death.

🎵 Experience

I

LIKE Crusoe with the bootless gold we stand
Upon the desert verge of death, and say:
"What shall avail the woes of yesterday
To buy to-morrow's wisdom, in the land
Whose currency is strange unto our hand?
In life's small market they had served to pay
Some late-found rapture, could we but delay
Till Time hath matched our means to our demand."

But otherwise Fate wills it, for, behold,
Our gathered strength of individual pain,
When Time's long alchemy hath made it gold,
Dies with us—hoarded all these years in vain,
Since those that might be heir to it the mould
Renew, and coin themselves new griefs again.

II

O Death, we come full-handed to thy gate,
Rich with strange burden of the mingled years,
Gains and renunciations, mirth and tears,

And love's oblivion, and remembering hate,
Nor know we what compulsion laid such freight
Upon our souls—and shall our hopes and fears
Buy nothing of thee, Death? Behold our wares,
And sell us the one joy for which we wait.
Had we lived longer, life had such for sale,
With the last coin of sorrow purchased cheap,
But now we stand before thy shadowy pale,
And all our longings lie within thy keep—
Death, can it be the years shall naught avail?

"Not so," Death answered, "they shall purchase sleep."

[?] (1893)

Oct 12. 1927

I will not think of you as dead, but one
Scattered like seed upon the autumn breeze
Renewing life where all seemed closed & comely,
Stored in ...

So that this Earth, this meaningless Earth, may yet
Regain some sense for me, because a word
thought trembles in the yet
Of the frail fountain at my garden's edge
Of the frail fountain in our garden close,
Because you paused one day before this urn,
Or a thought of ...

Or I can hear you in the migrant bird
croaking softly across the ivy-leaf
Before the asters fall on all
along the lime-tree aisle;
And feel your hand in mine, & breathe awhile.

Wharton's working draft of "Garden Valedictory," her elegy for Walter Berry.

Confronting a specific and devastating death when she was sixty-five, Wharton wrote this elegy for her dearest friend, Walter Berry, a man she met the same summer she was courted by Teddy Wharton. He was reluctant to propose to her, perhaps because he felt he had inadequate resources, but they remained loyal, lifelong friends, and his death crushed her. The draft of this poem shows much handling, revising, and perhaps her tears.

🜲 Garden Valedictory
October 12, 1927

I WILL not say that you are dead, but only
Scattered like seed upon the autumn breeze,
   Renewing life where all seemed locked and lonely,
   Stored in shut buds and inarticulate trees,

So that this earth, this meaningless earth, may yet
   Regain some sense for me, because a word
   You spoke in passing trembles in the jet
     Of the frail fountain in my garden-close,
   Because you stopped one day before this rose,
Or I can hear you in the migrant bird
   Throating goodbye along the lime-tree aisle,
     And feel your hand in mine, and breathe awhile.

[1927] (1928)

Although this sonnet was never published in her lifetime, Wharton left a typed manuscript of it, suggesting she had plans—or at least hopes—of publication. Beginning with a study of death, it turns after the octave to suggest, perhaps, acceptance.

❦ Death

LET me from death draw back a little space,
As from a stranger's face his host might lean,
To read its lines, and what is writ between,
Before awarding him his household place—
Yea, death, let me behold thee face to face
Before thou blottest all that I have seen,
That I may know thee when thou enterest in
Bearing thy covered cup of grief or grace.

Then shalt thou find me, at the worst, content
To have spoiled the spoiler of some matchless days,
Remembering how the joys that soonest went
Left in my soul the slumbering seeds of praise,
And glad of all the gladness that is spent,
As one who warms him in the sun's last rays.

[1889–93] (2019)

We don't know when or for whom this elegiac poem was written, only that it appears in rough holograph manuscript, with many crossings-out and substitutions, but essentially complete. Perhaps it was meant in the spirit of some of her supernatural poems and stories. Like her elegy for Theodore Roosevelt, it alludes to a myth about figures from the world of the dead who come to accompany a newly passed soul to its rest.

🐝 The Great Companions

GREAT SHAPES that stand about his door
And wait to lead him home,
Suffer that to his side once more
With silent step I come.

My breathing shall not stir a leaf
Of that full wreath You bear,
My tears disturb the filial grief
Of those who watch him there;

But as the hand that from his side
He never more shall raise
Once threw the gates of wonder wide
To my imprisoned gaze,

Showing me fields beyond our sheaves,
And seas beyond our sails,
And the long light that Beauty leaves
Upon her fallen veils,

So may it chance that now, before
The moment of his going,
My noiseless touch upon his door
Shall set the spring winds blowing,

The rustle of my soul's wings seem
About his sunken head
Like bird-calls through a morning dream
Before the East is red,

And of the light he gave, one ray
Turn back upon its traces,
Shine on the darkness of his way
And show your waiting Faces.

[?] (2019)

This wry little meditation on older age is undated.

🪶 Finis

WHEN I grow tired of books, what then?

The postman's ring, the doctor's call,
The damage done by the plumber's men,
The rise in wages, the mercury's fall,
Knitting-needles and crochet-hooks,
An afternoon nap in a nice warm shawl,
And now and then, as a special treat,
A funeral passing down the street.

That's the way the future looks
When I've grown tired of books.

[?] (2019)

This poem was found in a notebook dated 1932, the year Wharton turned seventy. By then she had lost numerous friends and family and suffered several heart attacks. She was contemplating her own death.

🦋 Lullaby for a Tired Heart

Iᴛ will go
Like the snow
That falls in March,
Like the glow
Of the rainbow's arch
In the sun,
The Tempest done . . .
It will go
As streams flow,
You the leaf
The stream carries,
With your grief
That's as brief,
On the tide that never tarries—
You will go.

[February 8, 1932] (2009)

Written in March 1937, this is the final poem published with Wharton's permission, requested by the publisher Carlyle Straub for an anthology in memory of Edgar Allan Poe. Notice the form: a variation on tail rhyme and on the sonnet, with a sestet followed by an octave. Form and substance create the perfect memorial for Wharton herself; the poem appeared shortly after her death.

🌿 Treasure

WHEN unregarding Death shall come,
Pick me up and take me home—
The long long way—
Compose my eye-lids, hush the noise,
And put away the broken toys
At close of day;

If underneath my cleansèd lid
One secret vision may be hid,
Let it be
A purple shallow over-leant
By emerald pines the wind has bent,
And, when the evening sky grows pale,
A single umber-colored sail
At sea.

[1937] (1938)

Acknowledgments

This project would have been impossible without the help of many, many people. First thanks go to the Wharton scholars Carol Singley, Donna Campbell, and Fred Wegener for suggesting that I work with Wharton's poetry and providing conversations about textual scholarship. Many other Wharton scholars have shared their research and knowledge. Julie Olin-Ammentorp has been consistently generous with her time, expertise, and information gathered over years, including notes on and copies of obscure poems from the war era, and most especially with her warm friendship. Laura Rattray has been a strong cheerleader and generous contributor from her vast Wharton knowledge and sharp-eyed perspective. Sheila Liming shared important information, including helpful scans, from her study of Wharton's library, and she and her husband, Dave Haeselin, cheerfully rescued my work from computer limbo. Other Wharton scholars have contributed their expertise, including Gianfranca Ballestra, who helped with ekphrastic poems, especially on Italian subjects; and Cecilia Macheski, Maureen Montgomery, and many of the other members of the Edith Wharton Society. This work also relies heavily on the prior work of many scholars, most notably Stephen Garrison, editor of *Edith Wharton: A Descriptive Bibliography*, and the brilliant and comprehensive catalog of Wharton's library prepared lovingly by the late George Ramsden.

The next group of people to thank are the knowledgeable and indefatigable staff at The Mount, Edith Wharton's house museum in Lenox, Massachusetts. The librarian Nynke Dorhout; the director of visitor services and all-around Wharton scholar Anne Schuyler; and the amazing executive director, Susan Wissler, to whom this volume is dedicated, are only three of the entire staff who have made this work possible by providing access to Wharton's books, opportunities to share work in progress, thoughts about Wharton's poetry, and a strong belief in the importance of this project. My fellow board members at The Mount offered encouragement all the way. The local historian Cornelia Gilder and her daughter, the writer Louisa Gilder, have provided insight into several of the poems, plus support and tea and cookies. Other researchers to thank include Alexandra Tinari, who helped with Old Norse and German mythology; Amy Golahny, who shared her knowledge of ekphrastic poetry; Elizabeth Leckie, who hopped on a boat and went to Murano to find and photograph a painting about which Wharton wrote a poem; Linda Hoddy, Brent Damrow, and Richard Floyd, who helped with biblical references; Richard Kopley, who offered his good thoughts and interpretations of some of the poems; and Bonnie Costello, who offered her crucial reminder that the most important thing is to look closely at the poems. The students Damiano Consilvio, Monidipa Mondal, and Rebecca Grubb provided textual work and interesting conversation about two of the poems. My hero Ron Ragusa saved the 95 percent finished manuscript when my computer had a "catastrophic failure."

A friend who deserves an entire paragraph to himself is the poet, biographer, translator, and teacher Peter Filkins, who answered numerous questions about poetic form, shared his interpretations of some of the poems, and patiently read and corrected the manuscript of this book. No one could ask for a more sensitive, careful, and generous reader.

Many institutions provided support in my archival research. The Lilly Library at Indiana University awarded me the Everett Helm Fellowship to use the collection, and the librarians there were unfailingly helpful. No Wharton research can be done without the collection at the Beinecke Library, Yale University, where the librarians and archivists always cheerfully find and deliver the documents you most need. I thank them for years of assistance. Williams College provided me with research and borrowing privileges, facilitated by Dave Pilachowski and Nicole Prokop. The Clifton Waller Barrett collection at the University of Virginia opened its holdings of Wharton materials. Other institutions and their librarians that provided materials include Aaron Lisec at the Morris Library, Southern Illinois University; Maria Victoria Fernandez at the Harry Ransom Center, University of Texas; Patrice Mattia at the Metropolitan Museum of Art; and unnamed librarians at the Hagley Museum in Delaware and Wellesley College Special Collections.

The novelist Claire McMillan provided a crucial contact for publishing, for which I shall be forever grateful. Julia Masnik of the Watkins/Loomis agency graciously navigated the complicated process of obtaining permission to publish Wharton's poems. Bill Flannery helped me to understand and negotiate the contracting process. Special thanks go to my editor, Ashley Gilliam, who received the idea of this volume with wonderful enthusiasm and supplied me with suggestions as to how to shape it; she answered every inquiry with an immediacy that was deeply reassuring, she has been my unfailing advocate, and her sharp-eyed, skilled editing improved the text. The copy editor, Jay Schweitzer, also improved the text, and I know there are numerous others behind the scenes making this a better, prettier book; I thank them all.

And finally, last but always first, I am endlessly grateful to the Wharton scholar Alan Price, who lived with Wharton's poetry patiently for years, reading texts and transcripts, sharing his research and thoughts, traveling with me to libraries, and generally being an excellent colleague and husband. I could not have done this without him.

Bibliography

Goldman-Price, Irene, ed. *My Dear Governess: The Letters of Edith Wharton to Anna Bahlmann*. New Haven: Yale University Press, 2012.

Moore, Charles Leonard. *A Book of Day-Dreams*. New York: Henry Holt, 1892.

The Nation [London]. Unsigned review of *Artemis to Actæon* by Edith Wharton, 1909, p. 577.

Smith, Logan Pearsall. *Afterthoughts*. London: Constable, 1931.

Wharton, Edith. *Artemis to Actæon*. New York: Scribner's, 1909.

———. *A Backward Glance*. New York: Appleton, 1934.

———. Diary 1926–1930. MS. May 12, 1926, Edith Wharton Collection. Indiana University, Lilly Library.

———. *Italian Backgrounds*. "Italian Backgrounds." New York: Charles Scribner's, 1905, pp. 172–212.

———. *The Letters of Edith Wharton*. R. W. B. Lewis and Nancy Lewis, eds. New York: Charles Scribner's, 1988.

———. Letter to Richard Watson Gilder, 3 November 1908, Scott Marshall Collection (Shari Benstock archives), The Mount, Lenox, Massachusetts.

———. *A Motor Flight Through France*. New York: Charles Scribner's, 1908.

———. Quaderno della Studente. MS. Edith Wharton Collection, Yale University Collection of American Literature, Beinecke Rare Book and Manuscript Library.

———. *Twelve Poems*. London: Medici Society, 1926.

——— [Edith Jones]. *Verses*. Newport: Hammett. 1878.

Wharton, Edith, and Robert Norton, eds. *Eternal Passion in English Poetry*. New York: Appleton, 1939.

Permissions

The following poems are reprinted with the permission of the Estate of Edith Wharton and the Watkins/Loomis Agency: "Dieu d'Amour," "The First Year," "Mistral in the Maquis," "Nightingales in Provence," "La Folle du Logis," "Les Salettes," "Segesta," "Treasure," and "With the Tide,"

The following poem is reprinted with the permission of the Estate of Edith Wharton and the Watkins/Loomis Agency and courtesy of the Yale Collection of American Literature, Beinecke Rare Book and Manuscript Library: "Lullaby for a Tired Heart."

The following poems are reprinted with permission of the Estate of Edith Wharton and the Watkins/Loomis Agency and with permission of Scribner, a Division of Simon & Schuster, Inc., from *Scribner's Magazine*, 1928. All Rights Reserved: "Garden Valedictory" and "Had I Been Only."

The following poem is published courtesy of The Mount, Edith Wharton's home, Lenox, Massachusetts: "[As birds from some green tropic gloom]."

The following poems are published courtesy of the Lilly Library, Indiana University, Bloomington, Indiana: "[A little while, My Sweet]," "Ame Close," "Avowal," "The 'Beata Beatrix' of Rossetti," "Beaulieu Wood," "Beaumetz, February 23rd. 1915.," "Beauty," "Cor Cordium," "Cynthia," "Dactylics," "Dante," "The Dead Wife," "Death," "Easter," "Faun's Song," "Gifts," "The Inferno," "In the Forest," "Latomia dei Cappucini," "The Leper's Funeral and Death," "Life [How sweet, O Life]," "Lucrezia Buonvisi Remembers," "Lucrezia Buonvisi's Lover," "The Masque of Life," "The Northwind," "[Not what we win but what we lose]," "October in Newport," "[O Love, let the world for once go by]," "A Patient Soul," "Penelope," "A Princess of the House of Este," "Renunciation," "The Rose," "Senlis. May 16th.," "The So-called Venus of Milo," "Song [Come, for the leaf is alight]," "Song [Let us be lovers to the end]," "Song [Mirth of life's blooming time]," "The Sonnet's Boundaries," "The Southwind," "Swinburne," "Terza Rima," "Two Days," "A Vision," "Weltschmerz," "[When I am gone, recall my hair]," and "[Words]."

The following poems are published courtesy of the Yale Collection of American Literature, Beinecke Rare Book and Manuscript Library: "The 'Apollo and Marsyas' of Perugino," "Esther," "Finis," "The Great Companions," "[I have had your love]," "Lullaby for a Tired Heart," "Martyrdom," "The New Litany," "A November Day," "The Oresteia," "A Picture by Sebastiani," "Sorrow's Sea—," and "Terminus."

The following poem is published courtesy of the Harry Ransom Center, University of Texas at Austin: "[She said to me: 'Nay, take my body and eat']."

Art Permissions

Page xxii. Yale Collection of American Literature, Beinecke Rare Book and Manuscript Library.

Page 78. Yale Collection of American Literature, Beinecke Rare Book and Manuscript Library.

Page 148. *Harper's Magazine* Vol. 103, November 1901.

Page 220. EdithWhartonsLibrary.org, courtesy of The Mount, Edith Wharton's home, Lenox, Massachusetts.

Page 234. Scribner, a Division of Simon & Schuster, Inc., from *Scribner's Magazine*, 1891. All Rights Reserved.

Page 238. Van Eyck, *The Virgin of Chancellor Rolin*: classicpaintings /Alamy Stock Photo.

Page 238. DaVinci, *Mona Lisa*: GL Archive/Alamy Stock Photo.

Page 244. Pisanello, *Portrait of a Princess of the House of Este*: Album/Alamy Stock Photo.

Page 248. Perugino, *Apollo and Marsyas*: Azoor Photo/Alamy Stock Photo.

Pages 262–63. Scribner, a Division of Simon & Schuster, Inc., from *Scribner's Magazine*, 1909. All Rights Reserved.

Page 310. Clifton Waller Barrett Library of American Literature, Albert and Shirley Small Special Collections Library, University of Virginia.

Index of Titles